WOMEN PATRIOTS
in the
AMERICAN REVOLUTION

Stories of Bravery, Daring, and Compassion

By Jack Darrell Crowder

CLEARFIELD

To the important women in my life:

Una, Ruby, June, Kay, Nancy, Peggy, Alicia, Caitlin, and Michelle

Printed for Clearfield Company by
Genealogical Publishing Co.
Baltimore 2018

ISBN 9780806358741

CONTENTS

Preface

7

Introduction

8

WOMEN PATRIOTS

BIBLOGRAPHY

Index

PREFACE

The role of women in the American Revolution has mostly been overlooked. Emphasis has been placed on the military and political activities of the men. These achievements would not have been possible without the contributions made by the women. They were the ones that kept the farms producing and moral high. Women faced dangers working as spies, they boycotted British goods, published writings in support of the American cause, and when necessary they defended their homes against attacks from the enemy.

The purpose of this book is to show the various roles the women played in their support of the war effort. Their contributions might seem minor to some people, but when they are seen in a single story there is no mistaking the importance they made in contributing to the victories on the battlefields.

The suffering of the men at Valley Forge, the British prison ships, and the long marches are well documented. However, women also faced daily pain and hardship. Many times they watched their homes burn, were threatened with physical harm, and buried their loved ones. Yet they never lost their spirit and determination.

This spirit was present in Beverly, Massachusetts on April 19, 1775 when the men in town left to fight the British at Concord. The women were left behind and alone, when one women said, *"None are left to protect us. If the regulars come during their absence, what will become of us, what shall we do?"* Another woman spoke up and with determination replied, *"Do? Who cares for the regulars? Let them come, and if they do not behave themselves, we'll take our brooms and drive them out of town."*

This spirit was still present on March 1, 1781, when just before his fourteenth birthday Bishop Tyler enlisted in the state militia. His mother helped Tyler put on his knapsack, and then she took his hand and prayed with him. When he left to join the troops her parting words were, *"Whatever happens to you never let me hear that you died of a wound in your back."*

This book is dedicated to the colonial women who were the secret weapons that the Americans had in the war effort. They were the weapons the British could not control or defeat. Most of these "Daughters of Liberty" are unknown and lost to history. For every act of courage reported in this book there are hundreds of courageous acts that will never be known.

INTRODUCTION

"Benedict Arnold, I come for my child. Not to ask for him but demand him of you." "Take him," replied Arnold. *"Take him, and don't you bring him up a damned rebel." "I shall take him,"* she said, *"and teach him to despise the name of a traitor."*

-----Mrs. Latham demanding her captured son returned

****

Women lost property and legal rights once they got married. Marriage and having children were the main goals for women. As a result, they were not expected to take part in the war. However, they did participate. They sewed uniforms, gathered supplies for the soldiers, and nursed the wounded. When the husbands were away fighting, they took over running the farms. Many of the women joined organizations that collected funds to assist the war effort. In 1780 over $380,000 was raised by these women's organizations.

Like the men, women held protests against British goods. The ladies of Edenton staged the Edenton Tea Party of 1774. They did not dump tea into the harbor like the Sons of Liberty in Boston, but rather they boycotted British tea and clothing.

At the start of the war George Washington was not fond of having women around his army. Mary Stiff applied for her father's pension (James McEwen R6700) in November of 1843. She stated in the pension that her mother told her, *"At one of the battles in which her husband engaged under Washington, that she handed Washington a drink of water out of a tin-cup & that he persuaded the women to get out of the way."*

Nursing was one of the first jobs that women had in the war. There were no trained professional nurses available to treat the Revolutionary War soldier. Most of the women learned about the treatment and care of the ill and injured from their mothers. In July of 1775 a plan was created to provide one nurse for every 10 patients and one matron, a woman who supervised the nurses, for every 100 patients.

The pay for the nurse was set at $2 a month, and the matron's was $4 a month. By using female nurses it would free up more men to serve as soldiers. The low pay for nurses and the exposure to deadly diseases kept many women from joining. The army encouraged camp followers to become nurses, and officers threatened to withhold rations from any woman who would not join.

Some women who were camp followers accompanied their husbands or family members when they enlisted. Some of these women sought adventure or were in search of a living. Most were involved in cooking, nursing, or doing wash. Occasionally, they fought alongside the men and were usually dressed as men, but they did not pass themselves off as males. There was no doubt in anyone's eyes that they were females.

A few women, however, went a step further. They disguised themselves as men and fought along with the soldiers. They knew that if they were discovered, they would be removed from the ranks and could face jail time.

Women made ideal spies because they were not considered smart enough to understand complex military strategy, so the men felt at ease to discuss plans freely around them. Also, women were able to move freely in and out of the enemy's camp preparing food, washing clothes, and selling various goods. While doing this, women would listen and observe what was going on with the enemy troops.

Molly "Mom" Rinker perched on top of a high rock in Fairmount Park in Philadelphia and knitted. As she knitted she observed British troop movements and dropped balls of yarn with the information to American couriers waiting below.

After the war many women hoped that they would gain more rights and equality. After all, they worked hard supporting the cause of liberty. Abigail Adams wrote to her husband John, who was working with others to frame the Constitution, to *remember the ladies.* More girls were allowed to attend school, and more women held jobs. Unfortunately, the rights of women and other minorities would be ignored for many years after the Revolution.

The work of the women on the home front and on the fields of battle were important to the successes of the Continental Army. The support of the women allowed the army to give its full concentration to the defeat of the British. Without the sacrifice of countless women, most unknown, the Americans would not have gained their freedom.

WOMEN PATRIOTS

Hannah White Arnett

Hannah was born on January 15, 1733 on Long Island, New York, and she died on January 10, 1823 in Elizabethtown, New Jersey. She married Isaac Arnett on May 6, 1753.

In December of 1776 a group of men met in Elizabethtown, New Jersey to discuss a British proclamation. Lord Cornwallis, fresh from a victory over the Americans at Fort Lee, was encamped at Elizabethtown. The British issued a proclamation that offered protection to all that would seek refuge under the British flag within sixty days and declare themselves British subjects. They would also be required to take an oath promising not to take up arms against the mother country or encourage others to do so.

A number of men in town met to consider taking the British offer, because it appeared to be good for several reasons. The American Army had suffered numerous defeats, England was the most powerful country in the world, and the majority of the American people were either neutral or against the break with England. For hours the debate went on between the men of Elizabethtown.

Outside of the room and listening to the discussion was one person that did not have a vote but did have a strong opinion. Hannah Arnett threw open the parlor doors and entered the room with her blue eyes blazing. *"Hannah! This is no place for you. We do not want you here just now,"* exclaimed her husband Isaac.

Hannah ignored him and addressed the men, *"Have you made your decision, gentlemen? I stand before you to know; have you chosen the part of men or traitors?"* The men were shocked by her boldness and tried to explain to her how hopeless the situation was. They reminded her that the American Army was starving, half clothed, had no discipline, and had been repulsed everywhere. *"We are ruined and can stand out no longer against England and her unlimited resources,"* they added.

Hannah then addressed the men, *"We are poor, and weak, and few, but God is fighting for us; we entered into this struggle with pure hearts and prayerful lips; we had counted the cost and were willing to pay the price, were it in our heart's blood. And now, now because for a time the day is going against us, you would give up all, and sneak back like cravens to kiss the feet that have trampled upon us. And you call yourselves men—the sons of those who gave up home and fortune and fatherland to make for themselves and for dear liberty a resting place in the wilderness! Oh, shame upon you cowards!"*

Hannah's shocked husband apologized to the men for his wife's outburst. The men in the room were quiet and were deep in thought. Hannah again expressed the confidence that England would never conquer the Americans. She added, *"For me, I stay with the country, and my hand shall never touch the hand nor my heart cleave to the heart of him who shames me."*

After she said these words, Hannah turned and faced her husband and in a stern voice she said, *"Isaac, we have lived together for twenty years, and through all of them I have been to you a true and loving wife; but I am the child of God and my country, and it you do this shameful thing I will never want you again as my husband."*

Isaac was shocked and replied, *"Leave me for such a thing as this?"* Hannah quickly replied with tears in her eyes, *"For such a thing as this? What greater cause could there be. If you take your protection you lose your wife, and I—I lose my husband and my home."*

Before the men left the room, they resolved to turn down the offer from the British and stand by their country through good days and bad.

Sources: 1. *Historic Elizabeth 1664-1932*, Warren Dix, editor, 1914, page 28. 2. Sons of the American Revolution application. 3. The American Monthly Magazine D.A.R., Vol. XII, January-June 1898, pages 1009-1012.

****

Mrs. Ashe

While British General Leslie and his troops stayed in Halifax, he and several of his officers were quartered at the house of American Colonel Ashe. At times, Mrs. Ashe would play backgammon with some of the British officers. One of the officers was the infamous Lt. Colonel Banastre Tarleton.

In 1781 Tarleton and his men were soundly defeated at the Battle of Cowpens. During the battle Tarleton and his men retreated, and they were pursued by Colonel William Washington. Washington caught up with Tarleton, and the two men engaged in hand-to-hand fighting on horseback. During the fight Washington slashed the hand of Tarleton. The fourteen year old Negro servant of Washington then shot Tarleton in the shoulder, and Tarleton turned and fired his pistol at Washington. The shot hit Washington's horse, enabling Tarleton to escape.

When Tarleton played backgammon with Mrs. Ashe he enjoyed using his sarcastic wit with her, especially using the wit at the expense of her favorite hero Colonel William Washington. On one occasion Tarleton jokingly said he would like to have the chance to meet Colonel

Washington, who he understood to be very small. Mrs. Ashe quickly replied, *"If you had looked behind you, Colonel Tarleton, at the battle of Cowpens, you would have had that pleasure."*

Apparently, the remark hit home with Tarleton, because his hand involuntarily moved to the hilt of his sword. The fact that a women said the insult kept him from taking his sword out. At that time General Leslie entered the room and noticed that Mrs. Ashe was clearly agitated. The General inquired why she was upset, and she told him the remarks previously made. The General replied, *"Say what you please, Mrs. Ashe; Colonel Tarleton knows better than to insult a lady in my presence."*

The biting remarks must run in the family for Mrs. Willie Jones, the sister of Mrs. Ashe, also encountered the sarcasms of Colonel Tarleton. Several months after the Battle of Cowpens Tarleton, in the presence of Mrs. Jones remarked, *"Colonel Washington, I am told, is illiterate, and cannot write his own name."* The witty Mrs. Jones replied, *"Ah! Colonel, you ought to know better, for you have evidence that he can make his mark."* Tarleton learned the hard way that a woman's tongue can be as sharp as his enemy's sword.

[Joseph Mathew wrote about Washington cutting the hand of Colonel Tarleton in his letter to support the pension application of William Scott. *"He* [William Scott] *has often shown me the Sword he said Colonel Washington cut out of the hand of Tarleton; Mr. Scott was near and seen it fall marked the place afterwards got it, he has kept it as a Trophy of war."*]

Sources: 1. *The Women of the American Revolution Vol. II* by Elizabeth F. Ellet, 1900, page 161. 2. *A History of the United States from the Discovery of the American Continent to the Present Time* by Benson J. Lossing, page 332. 3. Pension application W8706.

****

Agnes Hobson Bacon

Agnes was born July 4, 1740 in New Kent County, Virginia, and she died on October 8, 1799 in Columbia County, Georgia. She lived near Augusta, which became under British control in January 1779. In 1781 the Americans hoped to retake Augusta but were in need of reinforcements.

Agnes volunteered to take a message from Colonel Clarke in Georgia to General Greene in South Carolina. The enemy's line would have to be crossed, and if a man was sent he probably would not reach General Greene alive. With the papers safely folded in her bosom, she plunged into the swollen Savannah River on her horse. After she reached her destination she again crossed the enemy's lines, swimming the river on horseback, and riding many miles to return home.

Sources: *1. Revolutionary Reader, Reminiscences and Indian Legends* by Sophie Lee Foster, 1913, pages 284-287. 2. *Women Patriots of the American Revolution: a Biographical Dictionary* by Charles E. Claghorn, pages 17-18. 3. United States Magazine, Vol. III, No. 3, September 1856 by Virgil A. Lewis, pages 235-237.

****

Ann Bailey

At the time of the Revolution Ann was living in Boston, which was occupied by British troops in 1775 and 1776. Ann, disguised as a man, enlisted in the army as Samuel Gay on February 14, 1777 in Captain Abraham Hunt's Company of the 1st Massachusetts Regiment.

Recruits took no physical exams, and they just had to meet the minimum requirements. They needed to be fifteen years old, have a trigger finger, be at least 5'5" tall, and have a top and bottom tooth that met (for biting open a musket cartridge). Being a male was an understood requirement.

For three weeks Ann was able to fool the men around her. Bathing was not a requirement, and going to the bathroom meant going behind a bush. Ann did such as good job as a soldier that she was promoted to a corporal.

After three weeks Ann deserted, possibly because her identity was about to be discovered, or because keeping the secret and the strain of army life was too great. Captain Hunt issued an arrest warrant, and on March 3, 1777 he discovered that Corporal Gay was a woman. Posing as a man was illegal, and so she could be whipped, fined or put in jail. The court fined her fifty pounds and gave her two years in prison. A second trial was conducted, and the fine was reduced to sixteen pounds and two months in jail. After the trial she disappeared from history.

Sources: 1. *Encyclopedia of American Women at War: From the Home Front to the Battlefields, Vol 1*, edited by Lisa Tendrich Frank, 2013, pages 240-241. 2. *Women Soldiers in the American Revolution* by Mary Wienkop.

****

Ann Hennis Bailey

Ann was born in 1742 in Liverpool, England, and she died on November 22, 1825 in Gallia County, Ohio. She probably came to America as an indentured servant in 1761. Her first husband was in the Virginia militia and died in battle against the Indians in 1774.

She swore to avenge his death, and she began to wear men's clothing and taught herself how to shoot a gun. During the Revolution she served as a scout and messenger, and she became known as "Mad Ann" for her acts of bravery and heroism. She may also have acquired the nickname because the Indians thought she was possessed by an evil spirit.

On several occasions Ann left her seven year old son with a neighbor and rode around the area encouraging men to join the militia. She sometimes traveled between Fort Savannah and Fort Randolph, a distance of nearly 160 miles, carrying messages.

On her rides Ann often came across a group of Shawnee Indians. In one such encounter she was being chased by them and about to be caught, when she jumped off her horse and hid in a log. Though they looked everywhere for her and even stopped to rest on the log, they couldn't find her. They gave up and stole her horse. After they left, Ann came out of the log, crept into their camp during the night, and stole her horse back. When she was far enough away she began to scream at the top of her lungs. The Shawnee Indians thought she was possessed and could not be touched by a bullet or arrow. After this event they saw her often, but they feared her and only watched her from afar.

When Ann was interviewed she was asked if she was afraid of the Indians. She replied, *"No, I am not; I trust in the Almighty, I know I can only be killed, and I have to die sometime."*

When General Andrew Lewis's army was stationed on the Kenhawa River, Ann took her rifle, hung her shot-pouch over her shoulder, and led a horse laden with ammunition to the army over 200 miles away. She was selected for this task when a man could not be found to do it. When asked how she crossed the rivers, she answered, *"Some I forded, some I swam, and some I made a raft. I always carried an ax and a auger and I could chop as well as any man."*

She was asked what the General said when she brought him the ammunition. She responded, *"Why he'd say, you're a brave soldier, Ann, and tell some of the men to give you a dram."* [A dram was 1/8 of a fluid ounce of liquor.] She was known to be very fond of a dram.

Another story that may or may not be true is that Ann brought the first geese to Kanawha Valley. She was contracted by Colonel William Clendenin to bring him twenty geese, no more no less or he wouldn't pay. On the way back one died, so she put it in a bag and continued on. When he said he wouldn't pay because there were only nineteen, she threw the dead goose on the ground and said, *"There's your 20."*

When her second husband John Bailey died in 1802, she gave up her home and lived in the wilderness for over twenty years. She visited friends occasionally but often slept outside. A cave near 13 Mile Creek was said to be her favorite place to sleep. Ann continued to carry messages and supplies for settlers in the area. Her last trip was made in 1817 at the age of seventy-five. She died on November 22, 1825.

Sources: 1. *Women and War: A Historical Encyclopedia from Antiquity to the Present Vol. 2* by Bernard Cook, pages 46-48. 2. *Sketches of History, Life, and Manners in the United States* by Anne Newport Royall, 1826, pages 48-50.

****

<u>Penelope Pagett Barker</u>

Penelope was born on June 17, 1728 in Edenton, North Carolina, and she died in 1796. She married John Hodgson in 1745, and when he died she was just nineteen and had four children to raise. In 1752 she married James Craven, and he died two years later. Both of her husbands were wealthy, so she became the richest woman in North Carolina.

She married a third time in 1757 to Thomas Barker. He was forty-four and she was twenty-eight, and they had three children that all died before their first birthdays. In 1761 Thomas sailed to London, and he was unable to return home for seventeen years because of the English blockade of American ships. During this time Penelope ran the family business and became active in politics.

When British troops marched into Edenton they took Penelope's horses from her stable. In a fit of anger Penelope took her husband's sword off the wall in her home, raced outside, and cut the reins held by the British troops. The officer in charge, impressed by her courage, allowed her to keep her horses.

Penelope encouraged her neighbors and friends to stop drinking tea and using English products, until the tax on tea was repealed by the King. Months after the Boston Tea Party she wrote a statement that proposed a boycott on goods from England. She wrote, *"Maybe it has only been men who have protested the king up to now. That only means we women have taken too long to let our voices be heard. We are signing our names to a document, not hiding ourselves behind costumes like the men in Boston did at their tea party. The British will know who we are."*

Penelope and her followers, which numbered about fifty other women, created the Edenton Tea Party. The women met at Penelope's home on October 25, 1774 and signed the Edenton Tea Party Resolution which stated, *"We, the aforesaid Lady's will not promote ye wear of any manufacturer from England until such time that all acts which tend to enslave our Native country shall be repealed."* This may have been the first recorded women's political demonstration in the United States. Some of the women that signed the resolution are also in this book. They include Mrs. Robert Wilson, Rachael Caldwell, Elizabeth Steele, Margaret McBride, and Mrs. Willie Jones.

The group sent the resolution to a newspaper in London and hoped that it would cause an uproar in England. Newspapers and cartoons in English newspapers portrayed the women as bad mothers, loose women, and of both high and lowly stations in society. In the cartoon the women were depicted ignoring their children. A young unattended child is shown on the floor with a dog licking his face. It also showed the women enjoying themselves at a tea party while signing the document.

Penelope Ragett Barker and the Edenton Tea Party. British cartoon rom the book *The Boston Port Bill as Pictured by a Contemporary London Cartoonist, 1904.*

Men in London felt that the American women were stepping out of their expected gender roles. The Patriots in the colonies, however, praised the women for their stand against England. Other women began to boycott British goods in their support. English tea was then replaced with tea brewed from other herbs such as rosemary, thyme, sage, and mint. This tea became known as Liberty Tea. On January 31, 1775, Arthur Iredell wrote to his brother James Iredell, one of Edenton's leading patriots. Their sister, Elizabeth Johnston, was one of the signers of the resolution.

Dear Brother:

"I see by the newspaper the Edenton ladies have signalized themselves by their protest against tea drinking. The name of Johnston I see among others; are any of my sister's relations patriotic heroines? Is there a female congress at Edenton too? I hope not, for we Englishmen are afraid of the male congress, but if the ladies, who have ever since the Amazonian era been esteemed the most formidable enemies; of they, I say, should attack us, the most fatal consequence is to be dreaded. So dexterous in the handling of a dart, each wound they give is mortal; whilst we, so unhappily formed by nature, the more we strive to conquer them, the more we are conquered. The Edenton ladies, conscious, I suppose, of this superiority on their side, by a former experience, are willing I imagine, to crush us into atoms by American which possess so much artillery as Edenton. Pray let me know all the particulars when you favor me with a letter. Your most affectionate friend and brother." ARTHUR IREDELL

In addition to their protesting British goods, they raised money for the war effort and made clothing for the soldiers. Penelope continued to protest throughout the war. When her husband was able to return home in 1787, the couple built a new home.

Sources: 1. *Independent Dames: What You Never Knew About the Women and Girls of the Revolution* by Laurie Halse Anderson. 2. *Women Patriots of the American Revolution: A Biographical Dictionary* by Charles E. Claghorn, page 19. 3. *Women Heroes of the American Revolution: 20 Stories of Espionage, Sabotage, Defiance, and Rescue* by Susan Casey. 4. *The North Carolina Booklet*, by the D.A.R., page 332. 5. *The Boston Port Bill as Pictured by a Contemporary London Cartoonist* by R.T.H. Halsey, pages 313-322.

****

Kate Barry

Kate was born in 1752 in North Carolina, and she died in 1823. She married Andrew Barry when she was fifteen years old. During the Revolution she acted as a voluntary scout for the patriots of South Carolina. She was so efficient that the patriot bands were seldom surprised by the British.

Kate was a scout for General Morgan, who was also the commander of her husband's company of Rangers. Morgan found himself short of enough men in his army to give battle to Tarleton at the Cowpens. To alert the South Carolina Rangers, she swam her horse across rivers, evaded Tories, and was able to notify the militia that Morgan needed more men at Cowpens. As a result, the Americans were victorious at the Battle of Cowpens on January 17, 1781. It was a turning point in the reconquest of South Carolina from the British.

When she was captured by the Tories, she refused to reveal the position of her husband's company and she was beaten in retaliation. After the war Major Crawford told Kate's husband, Captain Andrew Barry, *"It is your duty to kill Elliot, the Tory who struck Kate with a whip to intimidate her and make her disclose where the patriots were encamped; but if you will not, then I will kill him, for no man shall live who struck Kate Barry."*

Captain Barry went looking for Elliot and found him at a neighborhood gathering. Elliot ran into a house and hid under a bed. Barry was allowed to enter the house with the promise that he would not kill Elliot. When Barry entered the bedroom Elliot came out from under the bed, and Barry grabbed a three-legged stool and hit Elliot with it. Barry then said, *"I am now satisfied, I will not take his life."*

Sources: 1. *Revolutionary Reader, Reminiscences and Indian Legends* by Sophie Lee Foster, pages 81-84. 2. *Women Patriots of the American Revolution: a Biographical Dictionary* by Charles E. Claghorn, page 20. 3. *The South Carolina Encyclopedia Guide to the American Revolution in South Carolina* edited by Walter Edgar.

****

Margaret Galbraith Barton

Margaret Galbraith was born in Virginia on January 24, 1752, and she died on June 24, 1828. She and her husband Roger Barton had twelve children.

When Margaret learned about a possible attack on Fort Statler by Tories in 1777, she rode her horse to warn the Americans. A government citation later given said, *"Margaret Galbraith, wife of Roger Barton, rendered an act of special services in the war by going at night with some danger to herself to warn a body of patriots of the approach of a number of Tories who were serving the British by betraying the whereabouts of their neighbors and others in the patriotic cause. They were thus able to disappoint the plans."*

Source: 1. Quote taken from *Women Patriots of the American Revolution a Biographical Dictionary* by Charles E. Claghorn, information submitted by Sue Malone Vardaman of Birmingham, Alabama, page 21.

****

Mother Batherick

On April 19, 1775 about 700 British troops under the command of Lieutenant Colonel Francis Smith were sent to Lexington and Concord, in order to capture and destroy rebel supplies that had been stored by the militia. British General Gage believed that reinforcements might be required to assist Colonel Smith. He ordered several regiments under the command of Earl Percy to leave Boston and march toward Colonel Smith.

Following in the rear of Percy's troops was a group of supply wagons that were having trouble crossing the Brighton Bridge. Word reached the rebels further ahead at Cooper's Tavern about the supply wagons, and the rebels began making plans to capture them.

Twelve rebels took a position behind a wall of earth and stones and waited for the groups of wagons. When the wagons appeared, the patriots called out for the British troops to surrender. The British tried to escape, and once the firing began the drivers jumped from their wagons and ran to the bank of Spy Pond. They threw their guns into the pond and then continued to run along the banks of the pond. They followed along the bank and met an old woman named Mother Batherick.

They surrendered themselves to Mother Batherick, who was digging dandelions. She led them to the house of Capt. Ephraim Frost, where there was a party of patriot men. She said to her prisoners, as she gave them up. *"If you ever live to get back, you tell King George that an old woman took six of his grenadiers prisoner."*

The following made the rounds in some of the British newspapers. *"If one old Yankee woman can take six grenadiers, How many will be required to conquer America?"*

Source: 1. *West Cambridge 1775* by Samuel Abbot Smith, 1804, pages 26-31.

****

Sarah Matthews Reed Osborn Benjamin

Sarah Matthews was born on November 17, 1744 in Goshen, New York, and she died at the age of 114 on April 20, 1859 in Mount Pleasant, Pennsylvania. She was married to her first husband William Reed, who died of a wound he received while serving in Virginia.

She married Aaron Osborn in January of 1780. Aaron had joined the army without the knowledge of Sarah, and when he did tell her, he asked her to go with him. Sarah refused, until she was promised transportation either on horseback or in a supply wagon. Aaron served as a drummer in Colonel Gansevort's New York Regiment and later transferred into Colonel Von Schaick's Regiment. Aaron and Sarah were discharged in 1783.

Sarah married her third husband John Benjamin in April of 1787. He also served in the Revolutionary War. When John died in 1827 Sarah never remarried.

On November 20, 1837, in order to obtain a window's pension and land bounty of 160 acres, Sarah gave the following deposition about her experiences in the war. Her grandson filed the pension application for her. Sarah is referred to as the deponent in the transcript,

"The deponent was married to Aaron Osborn, who was a soldier during the Revolutionary War. Deponent, accompanied by her said husband and the same forces, returned during the same season to West Point. Deponent recollects no other females in company but the wife of Lieutenant Forman and of Sergeant Lamberson."

"The Deponent was well acquainted with Capt. Gregg and repeatedly saw the bare spot on his head where he had been scalped by the Indians. Captain Gregg had turns in being shattered in the mind and at such times would frequently say to deponent "Sarah did you ever see where I was scalped," showing his head at the same time. Captain Gregg informed deponent also of the circumstances of his being scalped, that he and two men were out pigeon hunting and were surprised by the Indians and that the two men that were with him, were killed dead. But that he escaped by reason of the tomahawk glancing on the button of his hat. That when he came to his senses crept along and hid his __?__ one of the dead his dog came to his relief and by means of his dog the two fishermen who were fishing near the fort."

"Deponent further says that she and her husband remained at West Point until the departure of the army for the South, a term of perhaps one year and a half but she cannot be positive of the length of time. While at West Point deponent lived at Lieut. Foot's, who kept a

boardinghouse. Deponent was employed in washing and sewing for the soldiers. Her said husband was employed about the camp. She well recollects the __?__ occasioned when word came that the british officer had been taken as a spy. She understood at the time that Maj. Andre was brought up on the opposite side of the river and kept there till he was executed."

"On the return of the bargemen who assisted Arnold to escape deponent recollects seeing two of them, one by the name of Montecu, the other by the name of Clark. That they said Arnold told them to hang up their dinners for he had to be at Stoney Point in so many minutes, and when he got there he hoisted hos pocket handkerchief on hoisted sword and said, "now on boys" and that they soon arrived in Haverstraw Bay and found the British ship. That Arnold jumped on board and they were all invited and they went aboard and had their choice to go or stay---and some chose to stay and some to go and did so accordingly."

"When the army were about to leave West Point and go south they crossed over the river to Robinsons farms and remained there for a length of time to induce the belief, as deponent understood, that they were going to take up quarters there, whereas they re-crossed the river in the night time into the ferreys and traveled all night in a direct course for Philadelphia. Deponent was part of the time in a wagon. Deponent's said husband was still serving as one of the Company's guards---A man by the name of Burke was hung about this time for alleged treason but __?__ especially for insulting adjutant Wondell the prosecutor against Burke as deponent understood and believed at this time. There was so much opposition to the execution of Burke that it was deferred some time and he was finally executed in a different place from what was originally intended."

This author researched the man named Burke. I was able to find only two men hanged for treason in Pennsylvania around this time. One man, David Dawson was hung in Philadelphia, and the other man was Ralph Morden hung in Easton. Ironically both men were Quakers and both hung on November 25, 1780. There were only fifteen people put to death for treason during the Revolutionary War.

"In their march from Philadelphia they were under command of Generals Washington and Clinton, Col. Van Schaick, Capt Gregg, Capt Parsons, Lt Thomas, Ensign Clinton one of the General's sons [this was probably James Clinton, son of General James Clinton]. They continued their march to Philadelphia, deponent on horse back through the streets, and arrived at a place towards the Schuykill where the British had burnt some houses, where they encamped for the afternoon and night. Being out of bread, deponent was employed in baking the afternoon and evening. Deponent recollects no females but Sergeant Lamberson's and Lieutenant Forman's wives and a colored woman by the name of Letts. The Quaker ladies who came around urged deponent to stay behind, but her husband said, "No he could not leave her behind." Accordingly, next day they continued their march from day to day till they arrived in Baltimore, where deponent and her said husband and the forces under command of General Clinton, Captain Gregg, and several other officers, all of whom she does not recollect, embarked on board a vessel and sailed down the Chesapeake."

"There were several vessels along and deponent was in the foremost. Gen. Washington was not in the vessel with the deponent and she does not know where he was till he arrived at Yorktown where she again saw him. He might have embarked at another place but deponent is confident she embarked at Baltimore and that Gen. Clinton was in the same vessel with them as some of the troops went down by land. They continued sail until they had got up the St. James river

as far as the tide would carry them, about 12 miles from the mouth, and then landed, and the tide being spent, they had a fine time catching sea lobsters, which they ate."

"They, however, marched immediately for a place called Williamsburg, as she thinks, deponent alternately on horse back and on foot. They arrived, they remained two days till the army all came in by land and then marched to Yorktown, or Little York as it was then called. Deponent was on foot and the other females above named and her said husband still on commissary's guard. Deponent attention was arrested by the appearance of a large plain between them and Yorktown and an entrenchment thrown up. She also saw a number of dead negroes lying around their encampment, whom she understood the British had driven out of town and left to starve, or were first starved and then thrown out."

"Deponent took her stand back of the American tents, say about a mile from the town, and busied herself washing, mending, and cooking for the soldiers, in which she was assisted by the other females, some men washing their own clothing. She heard the roar of the artillery for a number of days, and the last night the Americans threw up entrenchments, it was a misty, foggy night, rather wet but not rainy. Every soldier threw up for himself, as she understood, and she afterwards saw and went into the entrenchments. Deponent's said husband was there throwing up entrenchments, and deponent cooked and carried in beef, and bread, and coffee (in a gallon pot) to the soldiers in the entrenchment."

"On one occasion when deponent was thus employed carrying in provisions, she met General Washington, who asked her if she "was not afraid of the cannonballs?" She replied "no, the bullets would not cheat the gallows, that it would not do for the men to fight and starve too."

"They dug entrenchments nearer and nearer to Yorktown every night or two till the last. While digging that, the enemy fired very heavy till about nine o'clock next morning, then stopped, and the drums from the enemy beat excessively. Deponent was a little way off in Col. Von Schaick, or the officers, marque and a number of officers were present among whom was Captain Gregg, who, on account of infirmities did not go out much to do duty, the drums continued beating, and all at once the officers hurrahed and swung their hats, and deponent asked, "what is the matter now?" One of them replied "are not you soldier enough to know what it means?" Deponent replied "no", they then replied, "the British have surrendered." Deponent having provisions ready, carried the same down to the entrenchments that morning and four of the soldiers whom she was in the habit of cooking for ate their breakfast. Deponent stood on one side of the road and the officers upon the other side, when the British officers came out of the town and rode up to the American officers and delivered up their swords which the deponent thinks were returned again, and the British officers rode right on before the army who marched out beating and playing a melancholy tune, their drums covered with black hankf's and their fifes with black ribbons toed around them—into old field and there grounded their arms and then returned into town again to await their destiny."

"Deponent recollects seeing a great many American officers some on horse back and some on foot but can not call them by names. Washington, Lafayette, and Clinton were among the number. The British General at the head of the army was a large portly man, full face, and the tears rolled down his cheeks as he passed along. But it was not Cornwallis. She saw the latter afterwards and his being a man of diminutive appearance and having crossed eyes."

19

The man Sarah describes having tears rolling down his cheeks was probably General O'Hara. The General represented the British at the surrender because Cornwallis could not be there due to "illness."

"On going into town she noticed two dead negroes lying by the musket house. She had the curiosity to go into a large building that stood nearby and there she noticed the cupboards smashed to piece and china dishes and other ware strewed around upon the floors and among the rest a pewter cover to a hot basin that had a handle on it. She picked it up supposing it belonged to the British, but the governor came in and claimed it as his said he would have the __?__ of giving it away as it was the last one out of 12 that he could see and accordingly presented it to the deponent and she afterwards brought it home with them to Orange Country sold it for old pewter which she has a hundred times regretted."

"After two or three days deponent and her husband, Captain Gregg and others who were sick or convalescing embarked on board a vessel from Yorktown not the same they came down in and set sail up the Chesapeake bay and continued to the head of Elk [River] where they landed. The main body of the army remained behind but came on soon afterwards. Deponent and her husband proceeded with the commissary's teams from the head of Elk leaving Philadelphia to the night and continued day after day till they arrived at Pomptons Plains in New Jersey they were joined by the main body of the army under General Clinton's command and they put down for winter quarters. Deponent and her husband lived a part of the time in a tent made of logs but covered with cloths and a part of the time at a Mr. Manuels near Pompton meeting house. She buried herself during the winter in cooking and serving as usual. Then said husband was on duty among the rest of the army and held the station of corporal from the time he left West Point."

"In the opening of spring, they marched to West Point and remained there during the summer, her said husband still with her. In the fall they came up a little back of New-burgh to a place called New Windsor and put up huts on Ellis's lands and again sat down for winter quarters, her said husband still along and on duty. The York troops and Connecticut troops were there. In the following spring or autumn they were all discharged. Deponent and her said husband remained in New Windsor in a log house built by the army until the spring following. Some of the soldiers boarded at their house and worked round among the farmers, as did her said husband also. Deponent and her said husband spent certainly more than three years in the service."

"In the winter before the army were disbanded at New Windsor, on the twentieth of February, deponent had a child by the name of Phebe Osborn, of whom the said Aaron Osborn was the father. A year and five months afterwards, on the ninth day of August at the same place, she had another child by the name of Aaron Osborn, Jr., of whom the said husband was the father."

"About three months after the birth of her last child, Aaron Osborn, Jr., she last saw her said husband, who then left her at New Windsor and never returned. He had been absent at intervals before this from deponent, and at one time deponent understood he was married again to a girl by the name of Polly Sloat above Newburgh about 15 or 16 miles. Deponent got a horse and rode up to inquire into the truth of the story. She arrived at the girl's father's and there found her said husband, and Polly Sloat, and her parents. Deponent was kindly treated by the inmates of the house but ascertained for a truth that her husband was married to said girl. After remaining overnight, deponent determined to return home and abandon her said husband forever, as she found he had conducted in such a way as to leave no hope of reclaiming him. About two weeks afterwards, her said husband came to see deponent in New Windsor and offered to take deponent and her children to the northward, but deponent declined going, under a firm belief that he would *conduct no better, and her said husband the same night absconded with two others, crossed the river at Newburgh, and she never saw him afterwards. This was about a year and a half after his discharge."*

"Deponent heard of him after up the Mohawk river and that he had married again. Deponent, after hearing of this second unlawful marriage of said husband, married herself to John Benjamin of Blooming grove Orange County whose name she now bears. About twenty years ago deponent heard that her said husband Osborn died up the Mohawk and she has no reason to believe to the contrary to this day. Deponent often saw the discharge of her said husband Osborn, and understood that he deserve a bounty in land in the __?__ country beyond Ithaca but her husband informed her that he sold his discharge and land together in New Burgh to a merchant residing there whom name she can not recollect."

"Deponent was informed more than forty years ago and believes that said Polly Sloat Osborn's second wife above mentioned died dead drunk the liquor running out of her mouth after she was dead. Osborn's third wife she knows nothing about."

Sarah stated in her application that her husband John Benjamin died ten years ago (1827) and she was now a widow. John also served in the war, but she knew nothing of his service. She was granted a pension of $88 a year *"because of her own personal service"* during the war. When Aaron filed for a pension, he failed to mention Sarah in his application.

Sources: 1. Pension Application W4558. 2. Tombstone

****

Elizabeth Gilmore Berry

Elizabeth was born in c. 1759 in Dublin Ireland, and she died on August 21, 1824 in Washington County, Pennsylvania. She came to America with her sister Ann in 1776 from Ireland. Some historians claim she met her future husband, John Berry, onboard the ship. Other historians say they met when both were at Valley Forge in the winter of 1777-78. John was ill and Elizabeth nursed him back to health. The couple married in 1780.

Elizabeth and her sister served as nurses at Valley Forge. According to a newspaper account, she later served as a private in the Pennsylvania Rangers and drew pay with other members of the company. According to family tradition, Elizabeth did not plan to be a soldier. She entered the service in place of her sister Ann.

Ann had dressed as a man and entered the service to be near her sweetheart Jack Strawn. Jack was killed and Ann begged her sister to take her place, so she could carry her lover's body back home to bury. Since the two girls looked very similar, Elizabeth agreed. Berry, also a soldier, did not know that the sisters had changed places and thought he was paying court to Ann, after waiting for her to stop grieving for her lover.

Elizabeth encouraged his attention, and they were married in 1780. Tradition says that it was only when they went to the Gilmore home while on furlough, that he realized the true situation, finding Ann still wearing black in mourning for Strawn.

Elizabeth later joined the Rangers to be near her husband. While in the Rangers she served as a scout and carried a rifle. After the war they bought 251 acres near McDonald, Pennsylvania from George Washington.

Sources: 1. Article in The Pittsburgh Press, Sunday August 2, 1953, page 98. 2. Article in the Daytona Beach Morning Journal, January 6, 1949. 3. D.A.R. Lineage Book, Vols. 50-60, page 175. 4. D.A.R. *American Spirit, Vols. 136-137*, page 38.

****

Katherine Montgomery Bledsoe

Katherine was born in Virginia in 1735, and she died in Tennessee in 1811. She married Captain Isaac Bledsoe in 1772 in Virginia.

On many occasions she carried important dispatches to General Washington, while traveling many miles on horseback in Virginia. On one occasion she encountered a British officer who rode with her for several miles. He told her it was dangerous for a lady to travel alone at such a time. She replied, *"Yes, but I feel no fear, knowing that no gentleman would molest a lady."* He complimented her on the beauty of her horse and with womanly tact she challenged him to a race. She was able to out-distance him so far, that she could safely deliver her dispatches.

Sources: 1. *North America, Family Histories, 1500-2000*, page 169. 2. Sons of the American Revolution Application. 3. *Women Patriots of the American Revolution: a Biographical Dictionary* by Charles E. Claghorn, page 29.

****

Susanna Bolling

Sixteen year old Susanna Bolling was not happy, when in 1781 Lord Cornwallis took over her family home to quarter his officers. One evening she happened to overhear the British officers discussing plans to attack the troops commanded by the Marquis de Lafayette. She knew where the American headquarters were located, and she decided to warn them of the upcoming attack.

In the cellar of the house was a tunnel that had been built in case of Indian raids, and it led to the Appomattox River. Susanna went through the tunnel, and at the end was a small boat by the river. She rowed across the river to a neighboring farm house and borrowed a horse. She quickly rode to the headquarters of Lafayette.

She was taken directly to Lafayette and told him what she had overheard at her home. Lafayette now had time to evade the British troops and to get a warning to General Washington. Soon after this event the British were defeated at Yorktown, and it is very possible that this young girl helped to make that victory possible with her warning.

Sources: 1. *Women Patriots of the American Revolution a Biographical Dictionary* by Charles E. Claghorn, page 30. 2. *Best Little Stories from the American Revolution: More than 100 True Stories* by C. Brian Kelly, page 116.

****

Jemima Boone

Jemima Boone was born on October 4, 1762 in Rowen County, North Carolina, and she died on August 30, 1834 in Warren County, Missouri. She was the daughter of the famous frontiersman Daniel Boone. The story of her capture by Indians shows the courage that young girls displayed on the dangerous frontier during the revolution.

When the Revolutionary War began, hostilities between the Native Americans and the settlers in Kentucky increased. Some of problems were encouraged by the British in the area. By the spring of 1776 less than 200 settlers remained in Kentucky. They were hiding in a few fortified settlements such as Boonesborough.

On Sunday July 14, 1776 thirteen year old Jemima, along with Betsey and Fanny Callaway, were in a canoe on the Kentucky River. A war party of two Cherokee and three Shawnee Indians captured the three teenage girls. Forced to climb the river bank, Jemima refused to move. She told the Indians that she would die before she would march barefooted. The Indians raised their tomahawks and threatened her, but still showing no fear she refused to move. The Indians finally gave in and gave her a pair of moccasins. The Indians took their captives north toward the Shawnee towns across the Ohio River.

Jemima and her two friends knew that their fathers and friends would discover that they were captured and would be on the way to rescue them. Jemima and the two teenagers did everything they could to delay the Indians. At times, the girls would fall down and complain that they had injured their leg or foot. Sometimes they complained that they were too exhausted to travel further and needed to stop to rest. Since Jemima was the main one slowing the party up, the Indians stole a horse for her to ride. When they placed her on the horse, she would without their knowledge kick, pinch, or prick the horse to get him to buck and throw her off. She continued to do this every time they placed her on the horse. The Indians soon gave up and set the horse free.

After the third morning of captivity, the Indians were building a fire to prepare breakfast, when the rescuers showed up. One of the Indians was shot and fell into the fire, and two others were seriously wounded during the brief fight. The remaining Indians made a hasty retreat leaving behind all of their equipment. One of the rescuers remarked, *"We sent them off almost naked."*

When the girls were returned to their homes, the settlers were surprised that the girls had not been abused. In fact, Jemima said that the Indians were kind to them considering the circumstances. Many years later Jemima said she bore no grudge against her kidnappers and even spoke favorably of their behavior. A few years after the rescue, Jemima married one of the men that rescued her, Flanders Callaway.

James Fenimore Cooper used this event as the basis for the captivity and rescue of Alice and Cora Munro in his story *The Last of the Mohicans*. The main character of the story had a strong resemblance to Daniel Boone.

Sources: 1. *Daniel Boone: An American Life* by Michael Lofaro, pages 68-74. 2. *Frontiersman: Daniel Boone and the Making of America* by Meredith Mason Brown, pages 106-110.

****

Margaret Louisa Smith Bowen

Margaret Smith was born in Virginia in October of 1737, and she died in Tazewell County on February 16, 1834. She married Rees Bowen in 1756 in Rockingham County, Virginia. Margaret was described as a small, neat, and trim woman weighing only about one hundred pounds. She possessed courage and a keen and resourceful brain.

Her husband Rees (Reece) was described as, *"a man of forceful physique, and his fame as a contestant in the fashionable fist fighting bouts of the day had spread far and wide."* It was told as fact that he could stand, and extend his arm, and hold her at a right angle to his body.

Prize fighting was very common in the settlements. The man who could beat all who challenged him was declared the champion and wore the champion's belt until someone beat him. Rees was the proud owner of the belt in the region. On one trip to visit friends, Rees and Margaret encountered a large man on the road dressed in buckskins. The stranger asked for the name of Rees, which was given to him. The man said he knew that Rees had the belt, and he challenged him to a fight.

Rees tried to postpone the fight, saying they were on their way to the home of friends and had their baby in his arms. The man called Rees a coward, and for the first time Margaret spoke up, *"Rees, give me the baby and get down and slap him in the face."* Rees gave the baby to a clearly agitated Margaret, got down and gave the man a severe shaking, and hit him several times in the face. The stranger left minus the belt, and the Bowen's continued on their way.

In 1776 Indians, perhaps stirred up by the British, began to threaten the settlement where the Bowens lived. The men had built a strong stockade in 1773 to protect their families. Fearful the Indians were heading their way, Rees and the rest of the men in the settlement decided that they would go out and attack the Indians before they reached the settlement. All the men left with the feeling that the women and children would be safe, since they would meet the Indians several miles to the north of the settlement.

After the men had left and late in the afternoon around milking time Margaret began to drive the cows home. While passing over some soft ground she discovered fresh moccasin footprints. The Indians had slipped by the men and were in the area. She knew what this meant, but she showed no sign of panic. Margaret went back to the stockade, fearful she would find the women and children killed and scalped.

She found that there had been no attack so she gathered the women and organized their defense. She told them to dress like men, get anything to use as weapons, and march around the stockade walls during the night. To her surprise, the other women out of fear would not do what she asked. The only person she could force was a large black woman.

Margaret dressed the woman in her husband's clothes, and she put on the clothes of her son. Margaret shouldered the only gun left in the fort, and she had the black woman shoulder a large stick. All night they marched around, where they could be seen from the woods. When Margaret's partner showed signs of fear and wanted to leave, Margaret said she would shoot her if she tried.

The next morning the men returned and discovered that the Indians had left. When the men went out looking for the Indians, they found on the hill overlooking the stockade the remains of the Indian's camp fire. Margaret and her second in command had prevented an attack on the settlement.

On October 7, 1780 Rees joined with the American forces and fought the Tories and British at the Battle of Kings Mountain. Rees, commanding a company, was killed in battle and *"was left in a hero's grave at Kings Mountain."* Margaret was left to raise eight children.

Sources: 1. Sons of the American Revolution application. 2. *History of Tazewell County and Southwest Virginia* 1748-1920 by William C. Pendleton, pages 387-390. 3. *Annals of Tazewell County, Virginia from 1800 to 1922 in Two Volumes* by John Newton Harman, Sr., pages 342-344. 4. *A History of Middle New River Settlements and Contiguous Territory* by David E. Johnston, pages 41 and 382-387.

****

Martha Bratton

Martha was born c. 1749 in Rowan, North Carolina, and she died on January 16, 1816 at Brattonsville, South Carolina. Her husband, Colonel William Bratton, was away fighting in General Sumter's army, and she was left in charge of the gunpowder hidden on their property. The British received a tip about the hidden gunpowder and rode to the Bratton house to seize it.

Martha learned the British were on the way and did not have time to hide it, so she decided to blow it up in front of them. She poured a powder trail some distance from the kegs of powder and waited. When the British arrived, she lit the powder trail and blew up the supply of powder.

The British became very angry and demanded to know who did this deed. Martha spoke up, *"It was I who did. Let the consequence be what it will, I glory in having prevented the mischief contemplated by the cruel enemies of my country."*

On July 11, 1780 she was paid another visit by the British who were looking for her husband. Martha told them that he was with Sumter's army. The British officer suggested that her husband should join the Loyalists. Martha defiantly replied, *"I would rather see him remain true to his duty to his country, even if he perished in Sumter's army."* The officer became angry at her reply and knocked her son, who was in her lap, to the floor. Another soldier took a reaping hook and placed it against her throat and threatened to kill her, if she did not tell where her husband was located.

She would not give them any information, and one of the soldiers persuaded the others not to kill her. The officer then demanded that she make dinner for them. After they ate the meal, the British went to another house to sleep for the night. Colonel Bratton returned home with about 75 of his men. When he learned that the British had been there he left and attacked them. Martha had her son hide up in the chimney to be safe from any stray shots. Several of the British were killed, some captured, and the rest escaped.

The captured soldiers and wounded were taken to the Bratton house. One of the captured soldiers was the man that asked that Martha's life be spared. Showing gratitude, Martha asked that the man be spared and not hung with the rest of the captured men. The man was later exchanged for an American prisoner.

Sources: 1. Tombstone 2. *Revolutionary Women: In the War for American Independence* edited by Lincoln Diamant, 1988, page 160. 3. *Heroines of the American Revolution: America's Founding Mothers* by Diane Silcox-Jarrett, 1998, page 23.

****

Elizabeth Burgin

Elizabeth was born c. 1740, and she died on January 22, 1832 in Allenstown, New Hampshire. One day an American officer asked for her help in planning an escape of American prisoners of war. She agreed and took the imprisoned men information about the escape and later assisted in the escape of over 200 prisoners on Long Island. Information about this event is from a letter that she wrote on November 19, 1779.

Elizabeth Town November 19 1779,

"July 17th being sent for by General Patterson, suspectd for helping the American prisoners to make their escape. George Hiblay coming from your Excellency the week before, and carried out Major Van Burah, Captain Crane, Lt. Lee, who had made their escape from the guard on Long Island, George Higby brought a paper to me from your Aide directed to Col Magaw on Long Island, he the said George Higby being taken up, and confined in the Provost guard, his wife told General Patterson that he carried out two hundred American prisoners for me, for which reason knowing myself guilty I secreted myself for two weeks in New York understanding that General Patterson had offered a bounty of two hundred pounds for taking me, he kept a guard five days at my house letting nobody come in our out. Through the behalf of friends I got on Long Island and there staid five weeks. William Scudder came to Long Island in a whale boat, and I made my escape with him, we being chased by two boats half way the sound, then got to New England, and came to Philadelphia. Then I got a pass of the Board of war to go to Elizabeth Town to try to get my children from New York, which I obtained in three or four weeks, but could not get my Cloaths or anything but my Children. When application was made by Mr. John Franklin my Cloaths and furniture, they should be sold, and the money be given to the Loyalists."

"I am now sir, very desolate, without money, without Cloaths or friends to go to. I mean to go to Philadelphia, where God knows how I shall live, a cold winter coming on. For the truth of the above your Excellency can enquire of Major John Stewart, or Col. Thomas Thomas. I lived opposite Mr. John Franklins, and by their desire make this application. If your Excellency please you can direct to Mr. Thomas Franklin in Philadelphia where I can be found. If the General thinks proper I should be glad to draw provision for myself and Children in Philadelphia, where I mean to remain. Helping our poor prisoners brought me to want, which I don't repent."

Some say she helped men on a prison ship to escape, but she never mentions a ship in her letter. The British commandant suspected that she was involved in the escape and sent for her. Elizabeth hid for two weeks while guards kept watch on her house, and a reward of 200 pounds was offered for her capture. She managed to make her way to Elizabethtown, New Jersey, where she sent for her children to join her.

Elizabeth had several people write on her behalf of the deed she performed. When she applied to the Board of War for the pass to Elizabethtown, the board replied that, *"From my representation of your character, your polite and humane conduct towards the American prisoners in general, and one in particular, he has promised to pay particular attention to your application and grant you anything in his possession were it possible."*

Elizabeth Burgin helped to free men like these from a British prison ship.

An American officer in Albany sent her a letter offering her lodging at his father's house along with 500 dollars, a promise that others would extend to her any funds or credit that she required, and *"a certificate of the kind treatment they recd from your hands."*

When General Washington learned of what she had done, he wrote to Congress on her behalf, explaining that, *"From the testimony of different persons, and particularly many of our own Officers who have returned from captivity, it would appear that she has been indefatigable for the relief of the prisoners and in measures for facilitating their escape."*

There are several statements that said she did aid in the escape, but there is no statement in describing what she actually did. Even so, Washington recommended to the Board of War in Philadelphia that Elizabeth be given free lodging in the city and food for her and her children. Elizabeth refused saying she did not want to be troublesome or expensive to the United States. She did say that she would like a job, cutting out linen into shirts, which the city purchased for the army. The city gave her the job and Congress voted to pay her a yearly pension of $53. 33. When the city first offered her food and lodging, she petitioned Congress,

The Petition of Elizabeth Burgin to Congress,

"That your Petitioner was a resident of New York, where she possessed everything comfortable about her, till the summer 1779 when she was rendered so obnoxious to the British Commanders, by her exertions in the service of the American Prisoners there, that she was at first under the necessity of concealing herself, & afterwards of flying in disguise to the people, an attachment to whose cause, had reduced her to a situation so unsuitable to her sex & age. What those exertions are, the services she rendered her country were, she leaves to be told by others. Mr. Franklin & General McDougall are not unacquainted with them, & His Excellency General Washington was sensible of them. That he addressed

27

Congress in her favour, and at the same time gave her an Order to draw Rations for herself & three small Children, till the pleasure of Congress was known. The Letter was referred to the Board of War, who kindly permitted her to occupy part of the House where the Office is kept, & have in some other respects assisted her, but her chief Dependance being on getting her rations, which from the scarcity of provisions, she could not at all times obtain, she was often obliged to sell part of what little property she had left to remove the misery and want of her hapless Family. As she wishes not to be troublesome or expensive to the United States, she humbly conceives if the Honble Congress would be pleased to direct her full employment in cutting out the linen into shirts, purchased in this city for the army, it would afford her a maintenance, until a happy change of affairs will permit her to return with safety to her native place."

Sources: 1. *Revolutionary Mothers: Women in the Struggle for America's Independence* by Carol Berkin, 2005. 2. *Heroines of the American Revolution: America's Founding Mothers* by Diane Jarrett-Silcox, 1998. 3. *Encyclopedia of American Women at War: From the Home Front to the Battlefields, Vol 1*, edited by Lisa Tendrich Frank, 2013, pages 112-3. 4. Papers of the Continental Congress, National Archives, Washington, D.C.

****

Nancy Butler

Nancy Butler was born in 1765 in South Carolina, and she died there in 1854. She helped to bury murdered American soldiers, while armed enemy soldiers stood ready to shoot the first person who attempted to give them a burial.

Source: D.A.R. Lineage Book, vol. 69.

****

Rachel Caldwell

Rachel was born in 1742 in Lancaster County, Pennsylvania, and she died on June 3, 1825 in North Carolina. She had memories, as a young girl running out the back door of her home as Indians were entering the front door with their tomahawks. Because of the danger of Indian attacks in Virginia, her family moved to North Carolina, a safer area of the country.

In 1766 she married Rev. David Caldwell, who for nearly sixty years was the pastor of the two oldest and largest Presbyterian congregations in Guilford County, North Carolina. Rachel and her husband ran a school, in which for forty years nearly all the professional men in the area and neighboring states attended. It was said that, *"Dr. Caldwell makes the scholars, and Mrs. Caldwell makes the preachers."*

Rev. Caldwell preached his opposition to British rule from his pulpit, and it resulted in a bounty of 200 pounds placed on his head by General Cornwallis of the British army. This forced the Rev. Caldwell to hide in a nearby swamp. Rachel was left to manage the farm, direct the school, and help with the duties of the church.

One day Rev. Caldwell ventured home, and it wasn't long before the house was surrounded by a group of armed Tories that took him prisoner. They were going to turn him over to the British but first they engaged in plunder of the home, which was the main reason they were there. The Tories had the plunder piled in the middle of the main room with a guard standing by Rev. Caldwell.

When the enemy was getting ready to leave, Mrs. Dunlap, a neighbor friend whispered in Rev. Caldwell's ear. She said, just loud enough for the Tories to hear, *"Was it not time for*

Gillespie, and his men to be here?" Immediately, the Tories began to panic and were afraid of being trapped. One of the men hollered, *"Let us go, or the damn rebels will be on us as thick as hell before we know what we are about."* The Tories ran from the house and rode off leaving their prisoner and plunder in the main room of the house.

Sometime during the fall of 1780 a stranger stopped at the Caldwell home and asked for food and lodging. He knew the home belonged to a preacher and felt he would be safe there. He told Rachel that he carried dispatches from General Washington to General Greene. Rachel was alarmed, because she was alone and knew that an attack from Tories could come at any time. She explained to the courier how her husband was wanted by the Tories, and staying at her home would be too dangerous.

Soon the two heard voices outside the house say, *"Surround the house!"* Outside the home was a group of Tories. The dispatches were too valuable to be allowed to fall into their hands. Also, the courier would probably be put to death and Rachel could be put in jail, or even worst she could be hung. She took the messenger to another door that led outside, and she told him to climb a large nearby locust tree and hide until the men had left. She then went back inside and out the front door to meet the men. She stood silently and watched as the Tories plundered her home.

Another incident with Tories occurred when they again raided her home and began taking everything of value. One of the scavengers broke open a chest and took out a tablecloth that had been given to Rachael by her mother. She grabbed it from the man, and they soon began to struggle over it. She was determined not to give up her heirloom. She turned to the other men watching the struggle and with tears in her eyes asked the men if they had wives or daughters would they want them to be treated like this. One man stepped forward, stopped the struggle, and allowed her to keep the cloth.

On March 11, 1781 Rev. Caldwell was off visiting the American camp of General Nathanael Greene. While he was away, a group of soldiers rode up to the Caldwell house and announced themselves as Americans. An older woman by the name of Margaret was standing outside, and said she was the landlady of the home and asked them what they wanted. The men said they wanted to see Rev. Caldwell. Margaret said he was at the American camp. Rachel then went outside, and the officer, identified himself as Colonel Washington and asked her the same question. The response was the same as before.

Both women were suspicious of the men and in the distance Margaret saw British troops marching toward them. She exclaimed, *"It's a damn lie! There are your damn redcoats!"* Rachel then asked to be excused for a few minutes while she tended to her children. She went inside her home and told some men hiding inside to escape out the back for the British were about to arrive.

When she rejoined the group out front, she was informed that indeed they were British soldiers and would need her house for a couple of days. Rachel, her children, and Margaret were told to leave the house and take up residence in the smokehouse. For several days they stayed there with no food other than a few dried peaches and apples. During this time the British ate and destroyed everything on the farm and in the surrounding area. They also burned the books and papers of Rev. Caldwell. In addition, they made it a point of insulting the women and children in the smokehouse.

A few days later a young British officer came to the door of the smokehouse to taunt Rachel by ridiculing her countrymen, whom he called rebels and cowards. Rachel's reply to these insults was, *"wait and see what the Lord will do for us."* The answer came on March 15, 1781 with the Battle of Guilford Courthouse, a bloody battle that gave the Americans a strategic victory. The British had a large number of casualties that led to the surrender of Cornwallis in October of 1781.

After the battle ended, Rachel led other women to the battlefield, and on that cold wet night they tended to the wounded. One officer, who had laid wounded for thirty hours, was found by an old woman. He told her that a Tory, who was a former friend, passed by him and refused to give him a drink of water. Instead, the Tory hit the wounded man. The woman tended to the wounded man who soon died. But justice was later served, for the Tory was later found dead, suspended on a tree in front of his own door.

After the war ended, Dr. Caldwell returned to his work as a teacher and preacher. Rachel aided him in his work, and she died in 1825 at the age of eighty-six. Her children were at her bedside when she died. She asked her youngest child for some water. As she raised up to drink the water, she sank back into her bed. She put her hands up and closed her eyes; then folded her arms across her breast, and with her next breath she died.

Sources: 1. *Women of the Revolution Vol. 1.* by Elizabeth Ellet, pages 150-158. 2. *A Sketch of the Life and Character of the Rev. David Caldwell, D.D.,* by Rev. E.W. Caruthers, pages 208, 210-224, and 269.

****

Deborah Champion

Deborah was born on May 3, 1753 in Gilead, Connecticut, and she died there on November 20, 1845. She married Samuel Gilbert in Gilead on 3 September, 1775.

In September 1775 she was asked by her father to deliver dispatches to General Washington in Boston, which was a distance of a little over 100 miles. In addition to the dispatches, she also carried the army payroll for the soldiers that had fought at Bunker Hill. Her father picked Deborah over her brother to carry the dispatches, because he felt that a woman would be less likely to be questioned than a man.

Deborah, dressed as an older woman, left early in the morning and was accompanied by the family slave, Aristarchus. Her mother had suggested that she wear an oversized bonnet that would cover her head and shield her face. This proved to be a wise suggestion, because when she was stopped by a British soldier, he let her pass saying that she was *"only an old woman."*

She rode through enemy lines and delivered the payroll and dispatches to General Washington. Before she returned home Washington complimented her on her patriotism and courage. Deborah later wrote of her adventure in this letter to a friend on October 2, 1775.

My Dear Patience,

"I know you are thinking it a very long time since I have written you, and indeed I would answered your last, sweet letter long before now, but I have been away from home. Think of it, and to Boston. I know you will hardly believe that such a stay-at-home as I should go, and without my parents too. Really and truly I have been."

"It happened last month, and I have only been home ten days, hardly long enough to get

over the excitement. Before you suffer too much with curiosity and amazement, I will hasten to tell you about it. A few days after receiving your letter, I had settled myself to spend a long day at my spinning, being anxious to get the yarn ready for some small clothes for father. Just as I was busily engaged, I noticed a horseman enter the yard, and knocking at the door with the handle of his whip, heard him ask for Colonel Champion, and after brief converse with my father, he entered the house."

"Soon after my mother came to me and asked me to go to the store in town and get her sundry condiments, which I was very sure were already in the storeroom. Knowing that I was to be sent out of the way, there was nothing left for me but to go, which I accordingly did, not hurrying myself you may be sure. When I returned, the visitor was gone but my father was walking up and down the long hall with hasty steps and worried and perplexed aspect."

"You know father has always been kind and good to me, but none know better than you the stern self repressment our New England character engenders, and he would have thought it unseemly for his child to question him, so I passed on into the family-room, to find mother and deliver my purchases. My father is troubled, is aright amiss, I asked."

"I cannot say, Deborah," she replied, "You know he has many cares and the public business presses heavily just now. It may be he will tell us." Just then my father stood in the door way. "Wife, I would spake with you."

"Mother joined him in the keeping-room and they seemed to have long and anxious conversation. I had gone back to my spinning but could hear the sound of their voices. Finally I was called to attend them, to my astonishment."

"Father laid his hand on my shoulder, (a most unusual caress with him) and said almost solemnly, 'Deborah I have need of thee. Hast thee the courage to go out and ride, it may be even in the dark and as fast as may be, till thou comest to Boston town?'"

"He continued, 'I do not believe Deborah, that there will be actual danger to threaten thee, else I would not ask it of thee, but the way is long, and in part lonely. I shall send Aristarchus with thee and shall explain to him the urgency of the business. Though he is a slave, he understands the mighty matters at stake, and I shall instruct him yet further. There are reasons why it is better for you a woman to take the dispatches I would send than for me to entrust them to a man; else I should send your brother Henry. Dare you go?'"

"Dare, father, and I your daughter? A chance to do a service for my country and for General Washington; I am glad to go."

"So dear Patience, it was settled we should start in the early morning of the next day, father needing some time to prepare the paper. You remember Uncle Aristarchus; he has been devoted to me since my childhood, and particularly since I made a huge cask to grace his second marriage, and found a name for the dusky baby, which we call Sophranieta. He has unusual wits for a slave and father trusts him."

"Well, to proceed, early the next morning, before it was fairly light, mother called me, though I had seemed to have hardly slept at all. I found a nice hot breakfast ready and a pair of saddle bags packed with such things as mother thought might be needed. When the servants came in for prayer, I noticed how solemn they looked and that Aunt Chloe, Uncle Aristarchus' wife, had been crying."

"Then I began to realize I was about to start on a solemn journey, you see it was a bright sunshiny morning and the prospect of a long ride, the excitement of what might happen had made me feel like singing as I dressed. I had put on my linsey-woolsey dress, as the

31

roads might at times be dusty and the few articles I needed made only a small bundle."

"Father read the 91st Psalm, and I noticed that his voice trembled as he read "He shall give His Angels charge over thee," and I knew into whose hands he committed me. Father seemed to have everything planned out and to have given full instructions to Uncle Aristarchus. We were to take the two carriage horses for the journey was too long for one horse to take us both, I riding on a pillion (a cushion). John and Jerry are both good saddle horses, as you and I know."

"The papers that were the object of the journey I put under my bodice, and fastened my neckerchief securely down. Father gave me also a small package of money. You know our Continental bills are so small you can pack away a hundred dollars very compactly. Just as the tall clock in the hall was striking eight, the horses were at the door. I mounted putting on my camlet cloak for the air was yet a little cool. Mother insisted on my wearing my close silk hood and taking her calash. I demurred a little, but she tied the strings together and hung it on my arm, saying, 'Yes daughter'. Later I understood the precaution."

"Father again told me of the haste with which I must ride and the care to use for the safety of the dispatches, and we set forth with his blessing. Uncle Aristarchus looked very pompous, as if he was Captain and felt the responsibility."

"The British were at Providence in Rhode Island, so it was thought best for us to ride due north to the Massachusetts line and then east as best we could. The weather was perfect, but the roads were none too good as there had been recent rains, but we made fairly good time going through Norwich then up the Valley of the Quinnebaugh to Canterbury where we rested our horses for an hour, then pushed on hoping to reach Pomfret before dark."

"At father's desire I was to stay at Uncle Jerry's the night, and if needful get a change of horses. All went well as I could expect. We met few people on the road. Almost all the men are with the army, so we saw only old men, women, and children on the road or in the villages. Oh! War is a terrible and cruel thing. Uncle Jerry thought we had better take fresh horses in the morning and sun up found us on our way again. Aunt Faith had a good breakfast for us – by candle light. We got our meals after that at some farm house generally. I left that to Uncle Starkey. As it neared hungry time he would select a house, ride ahead, say something to the woman or old man and whatever it was he said seemed magical, for as I came up I would be met with smiles, kind words "God bless you" and looks of wonder. The best they had was pressed on us, and they were always unwilling to take pay which we offered."

"Everywhere we heard the same thing, love for the Mother Country, but stronger than that, that she must give us our rights, that we were fighting not for independence, though that might come and would be the war-cry if the oppression of unjust taxation was not removed. Nowhere was a cup of imported tea offered us. It was a glass of milk, or a cup of "hyperion," the name they gave to a tea made of raspberry leaves."

"We heard that it would be almost impossible to avoid the British, unless by going so far out of the way that too much time would be lost, so plucked up what courage I could as darkness began to come on at the close of the second day. I secreted the papers in a small pocket in a saddle bag under some of the eatables that mother had put up. We decided to ride all night. Providentially the moon just past full, rose about 8 o'clock and it was not unpleasant, for the roads were better. I confess that I began to be weary."

"It was late at night or rather very early in the morning, that I heard a sentry call and

knew that if at all the danger point was reached. I pulled my calash as far over my face as I could, thanking my wise mother's forethought, and went on with what boldness I could muster. I really believe I heard Aristarchus' teeth chatter as he rode to my side and whispered 'De British missus for sure.'"

"Suddenly I was ordered to halt. As I could not help myself I did so. A soldier in a red coat appeared and suggested that I go to headquarters for examination. I told him "It was early to wake his Captain and to please let me pass for I had been sent in urgent haste to see a friend in need," which was true, if a little ambiguous. To my joy he let me go, saying 'Well, you are only an old woman any way.' Evidently as glad to be rid of me as I of him. Would you believe me – that was the only exciting adventure in the whole ride.

"Just as I finished that sentence father came into my room and said 'My daughter if you are writing of your journey, do not say just how or where you saw General Washington, nor what you heard of the affairs of the Colony. A letter is a very dangerous thing these days and it might fall into strange hands and cause harm. I am just starting in the chaise for Hartford to see about some stores for the troops, I shall take the mare as the other horses need rest.'"

"What a wise man my father is. I must obey, but I can say I saw General Washington. I felt very humble as I crossed the threshold of the room where he sat in converse with other gentlemen, one evidently an officer. Womanlike, I wished that I had on my Sunday gown. I had put on a clean kerchief. I gave him the paper, which from his manner I judged to be of great importance. He was pleased to compliment me most highly on what he called my courage and my patriotism. Oh, Patience what a man he is, so grand, so kind, so noble. I am sure we shall not look to him in vain as our leader. "

"Well, here I am home again safe and sound and happy to have been of use. We took a longer way home as far as Uncle Jerry's, so met with no mishap. I hope I have not tired you with this long letter. Mother desires to send her love."
Yours in the bonds of love.
   Deborah
"P.S. I saw your brother Samuel in Boston. He sent his love if I should be writing you."

Sources: 1. Deborah Champion, Letter to Patience, October 2, 1775. In the Miscellaneous Manuscripts Collection, Archival Manuscript Material, Library of Congress Manuscript Division, Washington D. C. Reprinted in Lisa Grunwald and Stephen J. Adler, eds. *Women's Letters: America from the Revolutionary War to the Present*, pages 25-28. 2. *Encyclopedia of American Women at War: From the Home Front to the Battlefield, Vol 1*. Edited by Lisa Tendrich Frank, page 131. 3. D.A.R. Lineage Book, Vol. 28, page 270. 4. *The Pioneer Mothers of America* by Harry Clinton Green, Mary Wolcott Green.

****

Ann Robertson Cockrill

Ann Robertson was born on February 10, 1757 in North Carolina, and she died on October, 15, 1821 in Nashville, Tennessee. At the age of fourteen she became the second wife of Isaac Johnston, who died a few years later when a tree fell on him. In 1780 she married John Cockrill.

In 1779 the fort in which Ann and Isaac lived came under attack by Indians and some British soldiers. The men were off hunting, so the women had to defend the fort alone. It was wash day at the fort, so Ann gathered the women and had them pass kettles of boiling water to her position on the fort's wall. When not firing at the Indians, she would pour the boiling water on them when they tried to climb the walls. During the attack Ann was injured several times, but she remained at her post until the fight was over.

After the death of her first husband, Ann and her three young daughters joined Colonel John Donelson and a group of settlers traveling to the Cumberland settlements by flatboat. At times Ann would serve as the pilot and steer the boat while the men would pole the craft upstream. The party arrived at their destination and established Fort Nashborough. In 1781, a year after her marriage to John Cockrill, the Indians attacked Fort Nashborough. Once again Ann helped in defending the fort. In 1784 she was the only female given 640 acres of land for her courage in the defense of the fort.

When she died in 1821 a granite tablet was placed on her grave with the following inscribed, *"Ann Robertson Cockrill 1757-1821, Intrepid Pioneer, Heroine of the Battle of the Bluffs, 1781, recipient of Land Grant."*

Sources: 1. *Women Patriots of the American Revolution: A Biographical Dictionary* by Charles E. Claghorn, page 50-51. 2. Tombstone.

****

Henrietta Maria Cole

Henrietta Cole was born on March 13, 1763 in South Carolina, and she died on February 17, 1854 in Pennsylvania. During the war she carried dispatches that contained important information.

Source: 1. D.A.R. Lineage Book, Vol. 39.

****

Polly Cooper

The Oneida Indians were one of the few Native American tribes that fought on the side of the patriots. The Oneida received word that Washington and his soldiers were starving at Valley Forge during the winter of 1777-78. The Oneidas had experienced a very bountiful harvest and had an excess of corn and other foods they could share. Chief Shenandoah of the Oneidas led nearly fifty of his men to Valley Forge carrying several hundred bushels of uncooked white corn. This amount was equal to about 70 pounds of corn per bushel. Among the Indians was an Indian woman, Polly Cooper.

The soldiers started to eat the corn uncooked, and they were stopped by the Indians. Eating the uncooked white corn could cause their stomachs to swell and kill them. Polly Cooper taught the soldiers the preparation process and the lengthy cooking time the corn needed so that the corn would be safe to eat.

Polly chose not to accompany the warriors when they departed for their homeland. Instead, she remained to help nurse the sick and to pass on her knowledge of medicinal plants and foods. She also served as the cook for General Washington and his wife Martha.

After the war the army offered to pay Polly for her service. She refused and told them that she was helping friends in time of their need. According to legend, Polly and some of the officers' wives took a walk in downtown Philadelphia to window shop. Polly saw a black shawl in a store window that she fell in love with. The wives told their husbands, and the shawl was purchased and given to Polly. The shawl still remains in the hands of her descendants.

Sources: 1. *Oneida Iroquois Folklore, Myth, and History: New York Oral Narrative* from the Notes of H.E. Allen and Others by Anthony Wayne Wonderely, Hope Emily Allen, 2004, pages 212-213. 2. *Encyclopedia of the Haudenosaunee* (Iroquois Confederacy) edited by Bruce Elliot Johansen, Barbara Alice Mann, 2000, page 65.

****

Margaret Cochran Corbin

Margaret was born on November 12, 1751 in Pennsylvania, and she died on January 16, 1800 in Westchester County, New York. She became an orphan at the age of five when her father was killed in an Indian raid and her mother was taken captive. She and her brother, who were not home during the raid, were later raised by an uncle. She married John Corbin in 1772.

When her husband joined the army, she went with him and became a camp follower. These were women who were paid to do the cooking and washing for the soldiers in camp. At times they would also take care of the sick and wounded.

They were at Fort Washington on November 16, 1776 when the British attacked. Her husband was a crew member of one of the two cannons defending the fort. Margaret dressed as man and helped her husband with the cannon during the attack. When John was killed, Margaret was standing by his side and took over the firing of the cannon during the battle. She had watched her husband clean, load, and fire the cannon enough times to know what to do.

During the battle she was hit by three grape shots which nearly severed her left arm, wounded her in the jaw, and wounded her left breast. After the battle, she and the other American prisoners of war were paroled, and she was taken to a hospital.

Because she was alone and disabled, she struggled to take care of her family. In June of 1779 Pennsylvania granted her a $30 payment for her service to cover her present needs. She joined the Invalid Regiment at West Point and aided the wounded until she was discharged in 1783. She married a wounded soldier in 1782. However, he died a year later. For her service she was given a pension for life equivalent to half that of a male soldier. She became the first woman to receive a military pension from Congress. When she died in 1800 she was buried at West Point.

Sources: 1. *Notable American Women, 1607-1950: A Biographical Dictionary Vol. II,* by Edward T. James, pages 385-386. 2. *Pennsylvania in the Revolutionary War 1775-1783. 3. American Genealogical Biographical Index Vol. 34,* page 310. 4. *American Revolutionary Soldiers of Franklin County, Pennsylvania,* page 49. 5. *D.A.R. Magazine,* August 1936, pages 778-779. 6. Pension File, Ancestry. Com.

****

Lydia Darragh

Lydia was born c. 1728 in Ireland, and she died on December 28, 1789 in Philadelphia, Pennsylvania. She married William Darragh on November 2, 1753 in Dublin, Ireland.

When the British occupied Philadelphia in 1777, they stationed soldiers in the homes of citizens. One of the homes belonged to the Darragh family. Lydia Darragh and her husband William were Quakers and therefore pacifists. However, their oldest son Charles fought in the Revolutionary War.

British General William Howe had moved into the house across the street from Lydia. She began providing her son Charles with information about the British troops by listening to talk around town and in her home. On the night of December 2, 1777 Lydia's home became the meeting place between General Howe and his staff. They were meeting to finalize the plans for an attack on Whitemarsh on the 4th of December, where General George Washington and his army was encamped.

Lydia told the British officers that she had sent her two youngest children to live in another city with relatives, and that she and William had no other place to stay and would like to stay in their own home. The officers knowing that Lydia and her husband were Quakers, and thus did not support the war, believed it would be safe to let them stay in their home.

The officers told Lydia they would meet in the parlor, and Lydia and William should go upstairs and go to bed. They told Lydia they would awaken them when they finished their meeting. Lydia pretended to go to sleep, but instead she listened to the officers through the door. She overheard them say they were going to make a surprise attack on Washington and would leave the city on December 4th.

She jotted down notes on what she heard, *"Howe leaving on 4th with 5,000 men for Whitemarsh, thirteen pieces of cannon, baggage wagons, and eleven boats on wagon wheels."*

Lydia quietly sneaked back to bed and pretended to be asleep when Major John Andre knocked several times at her door. Lydia got up and pretended to be sleepy and followed the officers to the front door of her house. She then extinguished the candles in the room and went to bed. She decided not to tell her husband of what she had heard.

Early that morning she told William she had to buy flour at Pearson's Mill. She was given permission by General Howe to cross British lines to go to Frankford to get her flour. Lydia walked three miles to Rising Sun, where she met Elias Boudinot, director of intelligence in Washington's army. Elias gave an account of his meeting in his journal,

"I was reconoitering along the Lines near the City of Philadelphia. — I dined at a small Post at the rising Sun about three miles from the City. — After Dinner a little poor looking insignificant Old Woman came in & solicited leave to go into the Country to buy some flour — While we were asking some Questions, she walked up to me and put into my hands a dirty old needle book, with various small pockets in it. surprised at this, I told her to return, she should have an answer — On Opening the needlebook, I could not find any thing till I got to the last Pocket, Where I found a piece of Paper rolled up into the form of a Pipe Shank. — on unrolling it I found information that General Howe was coming out the next morning with 5000 Men — 13 pieces of Cannon — Baggage Waggons, and 11 Boats on Waggon Wheels. On comparing this with other information I found it true, and immediately rode Post to head Quarters."

After her meeting with Boudinot, Lydia continued to Whitemarsh where she met Lt. Colonel Thomas Craig whom she knew. She also gave him the warning message, and then she made her way to the mill to pick up her flour and walk back home. The British later found the Americans waiting for them, and their surprise attack was foiled and Washington's army was saved.

The British knew that someone must have alerted the Americans ahead of time. One officer questioned Lydia and asked if anyone was awake the night of their meeting in her home. Lydia said only she and her husband were present, and they were asleep. The officer, satisfied with the answer, asked no further questions. Later Major Andre would report, *"One thing is certain, the enemy had notice of our coming, were prepared for us, and we marched back like a parcel of fools. The walls must have ears."*

Sources: 1. *Journal or Historical Recollections of American Events during the Revolutionary War* by Elias Boudinot, from his own original manuscript, 1894. 2. *All the Daring of the Soldier* by Elizabeth Leonard. 3. *Glory, Passion, and Principle: the Story of Eight Remarkable Women at the Core of the American Revolution* by Melissa Lukeman Bohrer. 4. Obituary in Pennsylvania Independent Gazetteer, 2 January, 1790.

****

Ann Simpson Davis

Ann Simpson Davis was born on December 29, 1764 in Buckingham, Pennsylvania, and she died on June 6, 1851 in Ohio. She married her childhood friend John Davis on June 26, 1783. John enlisted at sixteen and served in the army for more than five years.

Red-haired Ann was an excellent horsewoman, so it was not unusual for her Tory neighbors to see her riding around the countryside. At the age of fifteen she was handpicked by General Washington to carry messages to his generals, while the army was in eastern Pennsylvania. Many times she carried messages smuggled in sacks of grain and vegetables, in bullets, and in her clothing. She would deliver these messages at the various mills in and around the area. At times she would dress as an old woman, and more than once she had to swallow the messages when she was going to be searched.

Her service ended when General Washington left her area. Because she displayed uncommon bravery, she received a letter of commendation from Washington thanking her for her service.

Sources: 1. The Ann Simpson Davis Chapter, Daughters of the American Revolution. 2. Sons of the American Revolution Application. 3. Tombstone. 4. *Women Patriots of the American Revolution: a Biographical Dictionary* by Charles E. Claghorn. 5. D.A.R. Lineage Book, Vol. 116, page 90.

****

Catharine Martin Davidson

Catharine Davidson was born on May 16, 1768 in Northumberland, Pennsylvania, and she died c. 1816 in Pine Creek, New Jersey. She married Dr. James Davidson on March 31, 1785.

After the Tory and Indian massacre in the Wyoming Valley on July 3, 1778, the Americans fled to Fort Augusta near the home of Robert Martin. Catharine, ten years old, assisted her mother and younger sister in ministering to the wants of the fugitives. She took care of the sick and wounded who had crowded into their home and barn.

During the Great Runaway of 1779 she was again called upon to help in the relief of the many women and children who took refuge at Northumberland. This event was a mass evacuation of settlers from the frontier areas of north central Pennsylvania.

Sources: 1. *Some Pennsylvania Women during the War of the Revolution* edited by William Henry Egle. 2. *Women Patriots of the American Revolution: a Biographical Dictionary* by Charles E. Claghorn.

****

Mary Ramage Dillard

Mary Ramage was born c. 1755 in South Carolina, and she died there in 1795. She married James Dillard who served as a captain in the Revolutionary War. Records reveal that she was a beautiful woman, small, and very active.

Her husband was away serving in the army, when one evening British and Tory soldiers came to her home and demanded that she make them a meal. While serving the food she heard them discussing the upcoming attack on the American army in the area. When they left, Mary wanted to warn the Americans, but she had a small baby to deal with and nowhere to take him. She took the child into the bedroom, lifted up the bed post, and sat it down on the baby's gown. This would keep the child safe while she was gone.

Mary went to the barn and jumped on her horse without saddling it. Off she rode to alert the American Army. Her ride helped to prevent a Tory victory at Blackstocks on November 20, 1780, which became the first defeat for Colonel Tarleton in South Carolina. Some say she told American General Sumter that she would not tolerate any fighting on her property. According to family tradition, the British returned to her home, found the child, took him to a neighbor, and returned to Mary's house to burn it down.

On another occasion she was outside working when the British Army was marching by. As they went by she began to count the number of men in the army. When they were gone, she took the information to her husband who passed it on to his commander. Her spying was with risk, because her home was burned twice by the British and Tories. Mary died in 1795, probably sometime after the birth of her last child.

Sources: 1. *Carolina Herald*, March 1990 by Thomas L. Wallis, page 3. 2. *The Road to Guilford Courthouse: The American Revolution in the Carolinas* by John Buchanan. 3. Tombstone 4. D.A.R. Lineage Book Vols. 154-55, page 148. 5. Sons of the American Revolution Magazine, winter 2014, page 11.

****

Rachel Donelson

Rachel Donelson was born on June 15, 1767 in Halifax County, Virginia, and she died on December 22, 1828 in Nashville, Tennessee. In 1779 her father Colonel Donelson organized a group of flatboats to carry household goods, livestock, and 120 people to a new colony on the Cumberland River in Tennessee.

The trip took four months and covered nearly 1,000 miles until they reached Fort Nashborough on April 24, 1780. They faced frozen rivers, starvation, Indian attacks, and rapids on the dangerous journey. Along the way, thirty-two of the group died by drowning, illness, or Indian attacks. In 1781 the Indians attacked the fort, and Rachael assisted others in defending the fort. Young Rachel on numerous occasions had demonstrated her courage in facing the hardships of frontier life.

When she was around eighteen in 1785 she met and married Lewis Robards. However, Lewis constantly had irrational fits of jealous rage, and the couple separated numerous times. Because of physical abuse, Rachael left him for good in 1790. She fled to Natchez, Mississippi to stay with friends. A friend of the family accompanied her and served as her protector on the journey. She assumed that her husband would file for divorce after she left him.

In 1791 Rachel married the man that protected her on her journey to Mississippi, twenty-three year old Andrew Jackson. Two years later the couple learned that Rachel's first husband never filed for divorce. Later, research showed that a friend of Lewis Robards had planted a fake article in the newspaper saying that the divorce had been granted. When the divorce was really finalized in 1794, Andrew and Rachael were wed again in a small ceremony.

Jackson ran for president in 1828, and his opponents accused Rachael of being a bigamist and constantly attacked her character. Jackson won the election, but before he left for Washington Rachel died from what may have been a heart attack. Jackson felt that the unjust attacks on her during the campaign were the true cause of her death.

Portrait by Ralph E. W. Earl, 1823

Sources: 1. *Women Patriots of the American Revolution: a Biographical Dictionary* by Charles E. Claghorn. 2. *More than Petticoats: Remarkable Tennessee Women* by Susan Sawyer.

****

Betsy Dowdy

Betsy Dowdy was born in 1759 in Currituck County, North Carolina. In the fall of 1775 Virginia's last Royal Governor, Lord Dunmore, was losing his control over the colony of Virginia. He soon gathered his army of Tories and captured Portsmouth, Virginia, and then he took over Norfolk. These two harbors were important to British control over the colonies. He then traveled south and captured the Great Bridge in North Carolina. During this march his army burned homes and slaughtered the livestock. At the Great Bridge he built a stockade and installed two twelve pound cannons. The patriots called his stockade the pig pen. These actions by Lord Dunmore brought the war to North Carolina.

On the night of December 10, 1775 a neighbor visited the Dowdy's home and told the family of the capture of the Great Bridge. He told them of the burning of homes and killing of livestock. Killing the livestock especially alarmed Betsy, because she was fond of the wild horses that roamed the area. These were called Banker Ponies, which were descended from Arabian horses that were shipwrecked in the area several hundred years before. Over the years nature culled out the weak horses, and Banker Ponies emerged as a tough breed.

The neighbor said that a group of militiamen were on the way to the Great Bridge to win it back. However, the neighbor expressed doubt that they would have enough men to be successful. He went on to say that General Skinner was fifty miles south and had a hundred soldiers. If someone could take a message to him the General might get to the bridge in time to help the local militia.

Betsy went to bed but could not sleep. She worried that Dunmore's men would come to where she lived and kill the beloved Banker Ponies. She finally decided that she would ride the fifty miles and alert General Skinner and his men. She quickly got dressed and quietly left the house as her family slept. She mounted her pony Black Bess, and on that cold December night she headed south.

She and Black Bess swam across Currituck Sound, road through the Great Dismal Swamp, and then rode inland to the outskirts of Hertford where General Skinner and his men were camped. Cold and tired Betsy informed the General what had taken place at the Great Bridge. General Skinner called his men to arms and marched north. They arrived two days after the battle, which the colonial militia had won. The General and his men were welcome reinforcements, because the additional men meant that Dunmore would not dare attack the Americans again.

The ride of Betsy Dowdy has been compared to the famous ride of Paul Revere, with both being a dangerous ride. However, Betsy's ride occurred in the freezing cold of winter and not in the spring when Revere rode. Her ride covered 50 miles, and his ride covered less than 20 miles. With sheer determination and physical strength, this 16 year old girl and her pony completed a remarkable feat.

Sources: 1. North Carolina Booklet, Vol 1, September 1, 1901, No. 5. 2. *Women Patriots of the American Revolution: a Biographical Dictionary* by Charles E. Claghorn. 3. Betsy Dowdy Chapter of the D.A.R. Elizabeth City, North Carolina.

****

Phoebe Reynolds Drake

Phoebe Drake was born on August 28, 1771 in Westchester County, New York, and she died on November 21, 1853 in Dutchess County, New York. She married Jeremiah Drake.

Henry Reynolds, Phoebe's father, was a Quaker and an ardent defender of the cause of the colonies. He even took part as a soldier at the Battle of Stony Point. His outspoken support of the patriots caused hatred among his Tory neighbors.

Late one night the Tories broke into the Reynold's home and beat Henry. His pregnant wife entered the room, and seeing her bleeding husband on the floor she went into convulsions. One of the younger children, Caleb, entered the room and was beaten unconscious. Phoebe, only eleven at the time, fought the men with such fury that it took two Tories to restrain her.

One of the intruders put a rope around Henry's neck and hung him in the living room of the house. Believing him soon to be dead, they started to leave. Phoebe quickly cut her father down. The Tories threatened to kill her with a sword, if she did not get away from her father. She was stabbed with the sword, and she promptly threw herself on her father to shield him. She was then beaten with a rope, pulled from her father, and thrown across the room.

Once again the Tories put the rope around Henry's neck and hung him. As they were leaving, Phoebe again released him and threw herself on her father to protect him. Twice Phoebe was stabbed. The Tories took her father and threw him into a chest and closed the lid. Then, they looted the house and left.

Phoebe, now covered with blood, attempted to remove her father from the chest. Her mother had recovered and helped her get Henry out of the chest and onto the bed. Both were relieved when Henry's groan indicated he was still alive.

While Phoebe administered aid to her father, her mother shouted, *"Oh, Phoebe! Phoebe! The house is on fire in three places! And I can't put it out, if it burns down over our heads."* The Tories had set fire to some flax and two straw beds. Phoebe managed to put the fire out and tried to make her brother Caleb go to the neighbors for help. The poor injured boy was frozen with fear and would not budge. So, Phoebe left her home and started out to give the alarm to her neighbors. She warned her neighbors of the Tories, and a doctor was sent to the Reynold's farm. A group of armed settlers took out after the band of Tories.

Henry had over 30 wounds and fortunately none had hit a vital organ. One of his ears was nearly severed from his head, and one arm was so badly injured that he never regained use of it.

Sources: 1. *Women Patriots of the American Revolution: a Biographical Dictionary* by Charles E. Claghorn. 2. New York Times Article December 7, 1879.

****

Mary Draper

Mary Draper was born on April 4, 1719, and she died in 1810. She was the wife of Captain Thomas Draper of Dedham, Massachusetts. When news reached the town of the British advance on Lexington and Concord on April 19, 1775, the men grabbed their weapons to face the enemy. The women were active in their preparations of supplies for the men. These preparations continued over for several months when the colonial army surrounded Boston.

When Thomas left to join the army he was joined by his sixteen year old son. Mary's young daughter wanted her brother to stay home to protect the family but Mary told her, *"He is wanted and must go. You and I, Kate, have also service to do. Food must be prepared for the hungry; for before tomorrow night, hundreds, I hope thousands, will be on their way to join the continental forces. Some who have travelled far will need refreshment, and you and I, with Molly, must feed as many as we can."*

After Lexington and Concord, the Americans surrounded the British inside Boston for months. Many men would pass by the Draper house to join the army, and they all needed to be fed. Mary would make bread and cider for the men, and she kept a long table by the side of the road filled each day with food for the passing soldiers. Cider was served from several tubs and was dished out by several of the boys in the area. Each morning found Mary baking bread or milking her ten cows to provide for the soldiers. When she ran low of supplies, she would seek more from her neighbors.

In addition to the food she would also make clothing for the soldiers. She and her daughters would weave their own fabric, and they even used old bed sheets to make clothes. They made their cloth into shirts, pants, and coats for the men.

After the Battle of Bunker Hill in June of 1775, Mary heard that the men in the battle faced a shortage of bullets. General Washington had asked the people to send to his headquarters every ounce of lead or pewter they had so it could be melted down into bullets. Mary had a large supply of pewter, which she was a precious gift to her from her deceased mother. Before her husband had joined the army he had purchased a mold for casting bullets. Mary took not only her prized pewter but also her pans and dishes to melt down into musket balls.

It would have been almost impossible to sustain an effective army without the contributions of women like Mary. Their spirit and sacrifice made it possible for the men to continue fighting and eventually to achieve independence for their country.

Sources: 1. *Women Patriots of the American Revolution: A Biographical Dictionary* by Charles E. Claghorn, page 68. 2. *Women of the Revolution Vol. 1.* by Elizabeth Ellet, pages 115-118. 3. *The Part Taken by Women in American History* by Mrs. John A. Logan, pages 128-130.

****

Anna Elliott

Anna Elliott was walking with a British officer in her garden in South Carolina one day. The officer, noted for his cruelty and relentless persecution of those opposed to his political views, pointed to a chamomile and asked what kind of flower it was. Anna said, *"It's called a rebel flower."* The officer asked why it was called that. Anna replied, *"Because, it always flourishes most when trampled upon."*

Source: 1. *Daughters of America on Women of the Century* by Phebe A. Hannafore, 1883.

****

Rosanna Waters Farrow

Rosanna was born on June 1, 1734 in Westchester, Virginia, and she died in 1800 at Cross Anchor, South Carolina. Her husband, John Farrow died in 1776 from smallpox, which left her with five sons and three daughters to raise. The boys joined the American Army, and the oldest around twenty years old commanded a cavalry company. The youngest son, just a boy, served with the oldest son.

Mary was left alone with her three daughters surrounded by Tory neighbors. In times of danger Mary would take the girls and hide in the swamps or the woods. Many nights she slept with a pistol under her pillow.

During the summer of 1780, the British were having success in their battles in South Carolina. In order to discourage disloyalty to the King, American prisoners were sometimes put to death. One night Mary was awakened by a male voice at the front gate. She asked who it was and the man called back, *"Three of your sons have been captured in an encounter with the enemy and are confined in the jail at Ninety-Six, The British post. It's an unlucky thing, but Colonel Cruger is very anxious to secure the return of some of his redcoats that Colonel Williams captured at Musgrove's Mill and he sends word that he will give one rebel for two British soldiers if the trade is made in a hurry. It is said he wants to retreat from Ninety-Six and he will shoot or hang our boys when he does. I must go and tell all our people."* After giving the disturbing news he rode off.

Mary aroused her daughters, told them to keep all doors and windows closed, and to remain inside until she returned. She grabbed a musket, went to the stable, and saddled her seldom ridden horse. She got into the saddle as if she were a man, and she bound herself to it with a belt. As she rode away she yelled back to her daughters, *"It is not the most comfortable way of riding."*

She immediately rode to the American camp of Colonel Williams. She told him her story, and he released six British soldiers for a prisoner exchange and a guard for the prisoners. Before day break of the second night the small party reached the British camp under the command of Colonel Cruger. She used her apron as a flag of truce and explained to Colonel Cruger why she was there.

The Colonel replied, *"Well, you are just in time, for I had given orders for those rebellious youngsters of yours to be hanged at sunrise, but I guess you can take the rebels."*

"My sons!" she said with an angry tone in her voice, *"I have given you two for one, Colonel Cruger, but understand that I consider it the best trade I ever made, for rest assured hereafter the Farrow boys will whip you four to one."* As Mary marched off with her sons one British soldier half jestingly said, *"That's a pretty good speech for so dainty a lady, but she is as warm for the cause as the men."*

Sources: 1. *Rosanna Farrow – A Spartanburg County Revolutionary Heroine,* an essay by Miss Ruth Petty, Converse College, Class of 1897. 2. D.A.R. Lineage Book, Vol. 80, page 351.

****

Phoebe Fraunces

Phoebe was the daughter of Samuel Fraunces, a black West Indian. Samuel was a friend of George Washington and the owner of a tavern known as Fraunces' Tavern. The tavern became a gathering place for the Sons of Liberty and other patriotic groups. When New York City was occupied by the British, it became a hangout for British officers. In 1783 Washington gave his farewell address in its Long Room.

Did Phoebe Fraunces foil an attempt on the life of George Washington? Historians are not in agreement if the following story is true or not. It will be left up to the reader to decide the answer.

Washington and General Israel Putnam made their headquarters in a mansion in Richmond Hill about two miles from Samuel's tavern. Phoebe, one of the five daughters of Samuel Fraunces, became the housekeeper for George Washington. One of the visitors to the mansion was Thomas Hickey, who was one of Washington's bodyguards. Thomas Hickey was born in Ireland and came to America as a British soldier. When the Revolution broke out, he deserted to the American side.

At this time the British Governor of New York, William Tryon, was living on a British warship in the harbor. It is believed that Hickey had been "planted" to murder Washington and other high-ranking American officers.

Thomas became attracted to Phoebe, and she did nothing to stop his advances. Hickey told her of his plan to kill Washington by using poison. At dinner he wanted Phoebe to serve Washington green peas tainted with poison. According to one story, she warned Washington about the peas when she served them. Washington tossed the peas out the window and, according to legend they were eaten by chickens who promptly died.

Hickey and twenty others were arrested, and on June 28, 1775 he was hanged in Rutger's Square, becoming the first soldier to be executed in the American Army. It was said that a crowd of 20,000 people attended the hanging.

Sources: 1. *Recollections and Private Memories of Washington* by George Washington Parke Custis pages 411-412. 2. D.A.R. Magazine Vol. LII, No. 1, January 1918, page 11.

****

Aunt Betty Frazee

The Battle of Short Hills, also known as the Battle of Metuchen Meetinghouse, was fought on June 26, 1777. The fight was between the American General "Lord Stirling" and British Generals William Howe and Cornwallis. The Americans fought hard, but they were outnumbered, outgunned, and were forced to retreat toward Westfield.

While following the American retreat, Lord Cornwallis was near Westfield when he approached a farm house. The woman of the house, known in the area as "Aunt Betty" Frazee, was baking bread for the hungry American troops. Cornwallis approached her and said, *"I want the first loaf of bread that next comes out of that oven."* He then turned and sat under a large shade tree.

When the bread was done "Aunt Betty" took the bread to Cornwallis and told him, *"Sir, I give you this bread through fear, not in love."* Cornwallis was moved by her spirit and courage and told his men that none of them were to touch a single loaf of her bread.

Source: 1. *History of Union County, New Jersey, Vol. 1-2* by R.W. Ricord, 1897.

****

Mary "Polly" Worall Taylor Frazer

Polly Taylor was born in 1745, and she married Persifor Frazer in 1766. He served as a Lieutenant Colonel in the Pennsylvania Line. Two days after the Battle of Brandywine on September 11, 1777, Persifor was away spying on the British, captured by them, and imprisoned in Philadelphia. General Washington had earlier sent three wagonloads of officers' baggage to the Frazer house for storage. The house was located just seven miles from the Brandywine battlefield and twenty miles from Philadelphia.

Two days after the battle about 250 British troops arrived at Polly's house and demanded, *"Where are the damned rebels!"* Polly's children, servants, an injured American soldier, and a relative escaped the house and hid in the woods. Polly chose to remain behind and face the British.

The British entered her home and began to loot the house. They confiscated her liquor, and one drunken soldier was about to hit Polly when he was stopped by Captain De West. The officer said he was told that there was ammunition stored in or around the house. A search of the area found nothing, because the ammunition along with the baggage had previously been moved to other houses in the area.

Captain De West told Polly that the British would reward American officers that would join the British side. Polly laughed and said, *"You do not know Colonel Frazer, or you would not suggest such a thing, nor would he listen to me were I to propose it!"* She then defiantly added, *"If he did listen, and change sides, I would never consent to have anything to do with him!"* Seeing that they were getting nowhere with this obstinate woman, they stole things from the house, raided the barn of its wheat, and they took the horses.

Captain De West then told her that he had orders to capture her husband and burn the house and barn. He must have been surprised when she did not beg him to spare her home. He then told her that he would spare her property. She coldly replied, *"I cannot thank you sir, for what is my own."*

In October of 1777 she went to Philadelphia and took her husband and the other prisoners' food. During the winter at Valley Forge she took food, clothing, blankets, and over 300 pairs of stockings to the soldiers. On March 17, 1778 Colonel Frazer escaped from prison and was later promoted to General of the state militia by George Washington.

Sources: 1. *Mary Frazer: Heroine of the American Revolution* by Edward Owen Parry, pages 1-28. 2. *Women Patriots of the American Revolution a Biographical Dictionary* by Charles E. Claghorn, pages 80-81.

****

Elizabeth Freeman "Mum Bett"

Elizabeth Freeman was born c. 1742 to enslaved parents in Claverack, New York. When she was six months old, she and her sister were bought by John Ashley of Sheffield, Massachusetts. Elizabeth served Mr. Ashley for nearly forty years and became known as "Mum Bett." Her husband was killed fighting in the Revolution leaving her with a daughter called "Little Bett."

The majority of the slaves in Massachusetts were treated with almost parental kindness. They were welcomed into the family, and the duties of the master and servant were clearly defined. On the farm the master and servant shared in the work, and when finished they sat down to the same table to eat.

Colonel John Ashley was a Yale educated lawyer, and his home became the arena for many political discussions. He was the chairman of a committee that studied the grievances that the Americans in the area were working under. The result of the committee was a series of resolutions approved by the town in January of 1773. It was a petition against British tyranny and a resolution for individual rights. The resolutions were written by Theodore Sedgwick and stated, *"Mankind is a State of Nature are equal, free and independent of each other, and have a right to undisturbed Enjoyment of their lives, their Liberty and Property."*

"Mum Bett" by Susan Ann Livingston Ridley Sedgwick, 1811.

The Massachusetts Constitution was ratified on June 15, 1780. Its document included the following: *"All men are born free and equal, and have certain natural, essential, and unalienable rights; among which may be reckoned the right of enjoying and defending their lives and liberties; that of acquiring, possessing, and protecting property; in fine, that of seeking and obtaining their safety and happiness."*

45

Unfortunately, Elizabeth lived in the household of Mrs. Hannah Ashley, who was the exception to the rule of kind treatment. Hannah was raised in the less tolerant Dutch culture in New York, as she was described as *"a shrew untamable."* Every departure from her rule was criminal. It was said that, *"her justice was without scales, as well as blind."* Mr. Ashley, however treated the servants with kindness, and during this period of time the man's rule was supreme.

Elizabeth's sister Lizzy was sickly, and she was watched over by Elizabeth like a lioness watches her cub. One day in 1780 Mrs. Ashley was walking through the kitchen and discovered a wheaten cake. It had been made by Lizzy from the remains of a large wooden bowl, in which the family batch had been kneaded. Mrs. Ashley became enraged at the "thief," as she called Lizzy, and she grabbed a large iron shovel from the oven that was red hot. The woman raised it over the head of Lizzy, and when she swung the hot iron at the girl's head Elizabeth stopped it. She took the blow of the iron on her arm, which cut her to the bone. The resulting scar of the injury she would carry to her grave.

Striking a servant like this was not acceptable behavior in Massachusetts. Elizabeth had a bad arm all winter. Elizabeth explained, *"I never covered the wound, and when people said to me, before Madam* [Mrs. Ashley], *'Why, Betty! What ails your arm?' I only answered, 'ask missis!'"*

After the war ended, Elizabeth happened to hear the Declaration of Independence read at the town meeting house. There was similarity between this declaration and the resolutions written by Theodore Sedgwick. She had heard them before around the dinner table in the Ashley home. The next day she went to the office of Theodore Sedgwick and told him, *"Sir, I heard that paper read yesterday that says all men are born equal, and that every man has a right to freedom. I am not a dumb critter; won't the law give me my freedom?"*

These words would have been important to Elizabeth because of her longing for freedom. Many years later she said, *"Any time, any time while I was a slave, if one minute's freedom had been offered to me, and I had been told I must die at the end of that minute, I would have taken it, just to stand one minute on God's earth a free woman, I would."*

Sedgwick took her case, and he was joined by Tapping Reeve of Litchfield, Connecticut. Tapping later opened the first school to offer a comprehensive law curriculum in the United States. Since women had very limited legal rights in the country at this time, the two lawyers added another of Ashley's slaves to the suit. A male slave by the name of Brom was chosen.

Brom & Bett v. Ashley was tried before a county court in August of 1781. The jury found in favor of Brom & Bett, and they became the first African American slaves to be freed under the Massachusetts Law of 1780. Colonel Ashley had to pay court costs and thirty shillings to the defendants. After the court ruling Ashley offered to pay Elizabeth wages, if she would come back to work for him. Instead, Elizabeth went to work for Theodore Sedgwick as a housekeeper. She stayed with the family for years and became very loyal to them.

Elizabeth died in 1829 surrounded by her children and grandchildren. One of her great-grandchildren was W.E.B. DuBois the civil rights activist and writer. Her tombstone reads, *"She was born a slave and remained a slave for nearly thirty years. She could neither read nor write yet in her own sphere she had no superior or equal. She neither wasted time nor property. She never violated a trust nor failed to perform a duty. In every situation of domestic trial, she was the most efficient helper, and the tenderest friend. Good mother, farewell."*

Sources: 1. *Slavery in New England Bentley's Miscellany* by Catherine Maria Sedgwick, pages 417-424. 2. *African-American Social Leaders and Activists* by Jack Rummel, page 78. 3. *African American Lives* edited by Henry Louis Gates Jr. and Evelyn Brooks Higginbotham pages 317-318.

****

Sarah Bradlee Fulton

Sarah was born on December 24, 1740 in Dorchester, Massachusetts, and she died on November 9, 1835 in Medford, Massachusetts. She married John Fulton in 1762. Sarah and John would often visit her brother Nathaniel Bradlee who lived in Boston. John Fulton, along with Nathaniel joined a group of Americans patriots known as the Sons of Liberty.

On December 16, 1773 the two men, along with other patriots, dressed as Mohawk Indians and went aboard British cargo ships in Boston Harbor. The group of men dumped 342 casks of British tea into the harbor, in what became known as The Boston Tea Party. Sarah Fulton and her sister-in-law made the Indian disguises for the men and put war paint on their faces. The two women kept hot water in a copper kettle to wash the red stains from the faces of the men when they returned.

Sarah was also present with baskets of lint and bandages for the troops at The Battle of Bunker Hill on June 17, 1775. Because doctors were scarce, Sarah was placed in charge of care for the wounded American soldiers. At one point she removed a bullet from the cheek of a wounded soldier. She had almost forgotten the incident, until years later the soldier came by her home and thanked her.

In March 1776 Sarah agreed to carry a message through enemy lines from Major John Brooks to General Washington. She left at night, crossed a river, and returned safely by morning. Washington later visited the Fulton home and presented Sarah with a new ladle for her punch bowl. She served punch to Washington and years later served Lafayette from the same punch bowl, when the Frenchman visited her home.

On one occasion while Boston was under British control, her husband left to deliver a wagon load of wood for the American troops in Cambridge. The British stopped him and confiscated the wood. Sarah learned what happen, grabbed her shawl, and pursued the British. She overtook them, grabbed the oxen by the horns, and began to turn the wagon around. When the British troops threatened to shoot her, she replied, *"Shoot away."* Her defiant attitude astonished the soldiers, so they allowed her to take the wagon of wood.

Sarah died in her sleep at the age of 94. She is this author's 7th great grand aunt.

Sources: 1. Sons of the American Revolution application. 2. D.A.R. Magazine, December 1969. 3. *Boston Marriages from 1752 to 1761*, page 347. 4. *Women and War: A Historical Encyclopedia from Antiquity to the Present, Vol. 2*, Bernard Cook, page 212. 5. *An Encyclopedia of American Women at War: From the Home Front to the Battlefields, Vol 1*, Lisa Tendrich Frank, page 235.

****

Deborah Sampson (Samson) Gannett

Deborah was born on December 17, 1760 in Plympton, Massachusetts, and she died April 29, 1827 in Massachusetts. In 1782 Deborah disguised herself as a man and joined the 4th

Massachusetts Regiment as Robert Shurtleff. She served in the army as a man for nearly two years. Some accounts of her life say that she served at Yorktown. This is not true, because she enlisted months after the Siege of Yorktown.

Image of a 1797 engraving of Deborah Sampson from United States Department of Defense.

At the time she enlisted the British still controlled parts of New York, and Tory units raided in New York. Deborah was wounded in a Tory ambush near Tarrytown, New York. She received a head wound from a sabre slash, and she was shot in the upper front thigh. In order to keep her sex a secret she removed the musket ball from her leg with her knife. Her true sex was discovered when she was ill during an epidemic in Philadelphia. She was taken to a hospital when she lost consciousness, and the doctor that treated her made the discovery.

Deborah received an honorable discharge on October 23, 1783. She returned home to Massachusetts, and on April 7, 1785 she married Benjamin Gannett. To earn money she began a speaking tour in 1802 telling about her experiences. She was the first woman in the United States to go on a speaking tour. She and her husband continued to have financial problems, and at one point she even borrowed $10.00 from Paul Revere. Mr. Revere used his influence to get the Massachusetts Legislature to grant her thirty-four pounds for her service.

When she died her husband petitioned Congress and received a pension for her service during the Revolution. Unfortunately, he died before receiving it. In 1983 the Governor of Massachusetts declared that Deborah was the Official Heroine of Massachusetts. It was the first time in the history of the United States that any state proclaimed anyone as the official hero or heroine.

Sources: 1. *The Female Review: Or, Memoirs of an American Young Lady* by H. Mann, 1797. 2. The New York Times, October 6, 1998. 3. Sons of the American Revolution Application.

****

Emily Geiger

In the summer of 1781 in South Carolina General Greene called for a volunteer messenger to carry a letter to General Sumter, but because the area was swarming with Tories no one volunteered. *"May I carry the letter,"* said sixteen year old Emily Geiger. *"They won't hurt a young girl. I am sure, and I know the way,"* she added. General Greene had no choice, so he gave the letter to the young girl and also suggested she memorize it in case she was captured. Emily mounted her horse and off she rode sidesaddle.

On the second day of her ride she encountered three Tory scouts who stopped her and took her prisoner. She was taken to the Tory commander, Lord Rawdon, who in turn took her with her guards to a Tory home several miles away. In the home was Mrs. Buxton and her daughter, and both pretended to be Tory sympathizers because the area was thick with the cruel Tories.

Many years later in 1849 Mrs. Buxton's daughter recalled her meeting with Emily Geiger,

"I went with mother," she said, *"to see a woman prisoner. The door of the house was guarded by the younger scout, who was Peter Simons, son of a neighbor two miles away, and a right gallant young fellow he was. After the war he married my sister. I saw the young girl and I helped mother search her. We were amazed when we saw, instead of a brazen-faced, middle-aged woman, as we supposed a spy must be, a sweet young girl about my own age, looking as innocent as a pigeon. Our sympathies were with her, but mother performed her duty faithfully. We found nothing on her person that would afford a suspicion that she was a spy."*

They found no message, because when Emily was first brought into the house she was left alone by her guard for a few minutes. This was just enough time for her to tear up the General's letter and eat it piece by piece. Emily was thankful she memorized the letter, before starting the ride, in the event she was captured.

The scouts had no choice but to release the young girl. Mrs. Buxton gave Emily some refreshments and encouraged the young girl to stay on until morning. Emily politely refused saying that because the two armies were in the area, and she should ride on to her friend's house while it was still safe. Her guard Peter Simons, who was probably smitten with Emily's beauty, offered to escort Emily to her friend's house. Again, she politely declined the invitation and rode off.

She later reached the camp of General Sumter and delivered the message almost word for word. Her ride had lasted three days and had taken her through swamps and forests. She took very little time to rest. General Sumter immediately marched his men to join with General Greene, and once they joined forces the British under Lord Rowdon were compelled to retreat.

After Emily had returned to her home, General Greene presented her with a pair of earrings and a breastpin. Years after the war ended, General Lafayette visited the United States and presented Emily with a silk shawl. A grand ball was given in Lafayette's honor in Charlestown and Emily was present, and the two danced the first minuet together.

Many years after Emily's ride, she visited the house in which she was searched. She thanked Mrs. Buxton for her kindness on that memorable day. Also, present was Mrs. Buxton's daughter who had married Emily's captor, Peter Simons. Emily and Peter compared stories of that long ago day. Emily remarked that he was foolish to leave her unguarded for those few minutes, which gave her time to eat the message. Years later Peter Simons's son and Emily Geiger's daughter married.

Sources: 1. *Women of the American Revolution* by Elizabeth Ellet, 1848. 2. *The Percy Anecdotes* by Thomas Byerly and Joseph Clinton Robertson, Vol. 2, page 155, 1834. 3. *Women Patriots of the American Revolution: a Biographical Dictionary* by Charles E. Claghorn. 4. *Five Hundred Plus Revolutionary War Obituaries and Death Notices* by Mary Harrell-Sesniak.

****

<u>Mary Katherine Goddard</u>

Mary Goddard lost her father at an early age. To make a living she, her mother, and brother learned the printing trade. They were the first to publish a newspaper in Providence, Rhode Island. Her brother William left Rhode Island to start a newspaper in Philadelphia. William was also the publisher of the *Maryland Journal* which Mary took control of in 1774. She continued to publish it weekly for the next ten years.

After the Battles of Lexington and Concord she wrote details of the fighting, and on June 14, 1775 she stated in an editorial, *"The ever memorable 19th of April gave a conclusive answer to the questions of American freedom. What think ye of Congress now?"* She expressed to the British that the Americans would rather die than be slaves.

Mary Katherine Goddard from
Enoch Pratt Free Library

On July 12, 1775 she printed an account of the Battle of Bunker Hill less than a month after it occurred. Due to the slow spread of news this account could be considered a newspaper scoop. Later, that year she became postmaster of the Baltimore post office.

When the Declaration of Independence was written, the Founding Fathers first asked John Dunlap to print 200 copies of the document. The only names on this printed version were John Hancock and Secretary Charles Thomson, who is listed as a witness. There are 25 known copies still in existence.

On January 18, 1777 the Second Continental Congress moved that the Declaration of Independence with all the signatories be printed and distributed. Mary Goddard offered her press for the task. Congress consented, and her press became the second to print the document and the first to contain typeset names of signatories. At the bottom she printed, "Baltimore, in Maryland: Printed by Mary Katharine Goddard." By printing her name at the bottom she knew she placed her life in danger. [Though she printed her name Katharine, nearly every historian spells her name Katherine.]

That same year she printed a satirical article implying that *"we should do as the British say"* and signed it "Tom Tell-Truth." Satire often uses irony, which means you say one thing but mean the opposite. Some Patriots did not see the satire in the article, and they demanded that Mary tell them who wrote the article. When she refused to divulge her source, they wanted to shut her paper down. They stopped their demands when the governor spoke out on her behalf. Today journalists still believe in the right not to disclose their source for a story. [Many historians say that the author of the satire was Samuel Chase, a signer of the Declaration of Independence.]

As postmaster she kept exceptional records and, she established a delivery service rather than having people call for their letters at the post office. In one newspaper edition when ran the following ad, *"A Penny-Post wanted. A man of good character, well qualified to perform the business, or Letter-Carrier in this Town, will meet with good encouragement by applying to M.K. Goddard, at the Post Office."*

In 1784 she had a falling out with her brother, and William took over the newspaper. In 1789 Mary was replaced as postmaster despite a protest from many in the community. The reason given was the job required more traveling than a woman could undertake. Postmaster General Samuel Osgood replaced her with a political ally of his. For the next few years she ran a bookshop that was next to her newspaper and sold books, stationary, and dry goods.

Mary died on August 12, 1816, and in her will she freed her slave Belinda Starling who had been with her for many years. In her will she stated she left everything she owned to Belinda. *"I leave all the property of which I may die possessed, all of which I do to recompense the faithful performance of duties to me."*

Source: 1. *Encyclopedia of the Age of Political Revolutions and New Ideologies, 1760-1815* edited by Gregory Fremont-Barnes, page 310. 2. *The Amiable Baltimoreans* by Francis F. Beirne, pages 132-144. 3. *From Colonies to Country, 1735-1791* by Joy Hakim, pages 140-141.

****

Hannah Gorton

Hannah Gorton was born on September 16, 1770 in Rhode Island, and she died on May 6, 1863 in Providence, Rhode Island. Her father was a Lieutenant in the Rhode Island Militia. In the summer of 1779, at the age of eight, she carried water to the soldiers, fed them, changed their bandages, and washed their hands and faces. If caught aiding the rebels a person could be beaten, have their property taken or killed. Years later Hannah married Jonathan Hill who became a Captain in the Rhode Island Militia.

Sources: 1. Census of 1850. 2. *Women Patriots of the American Revolution: a Biographical Dictionary* by Charles E. Claghorn.

****

Elizabeth Hager

Elizabeth was born c. 1750 in Boston, and she died c. 1843 in Philadelphia. She was also referred to as "Handy Betty" or "Betsy the Blacksmith", because of her ability to use almost any kind of tool. Her parents were poor, and they died when she was about nine years old. As was the custom, she was "bound out" to a farmer living outside of Boston. This meant that she must work for the farmer until she was of legal age. In return the farmer would provide her with food, clothing, and shelter.

Besides the usual work around the farm, Betsy became an expert at weaving, and she could repair any part of it. She was described as very handy around tools, as strong as a man, medium size, and modest in temper. When the Revolution began, she was working for Samuel Leverett who was a blacksmith and farmer. Samuel was also very outspoken in his support of the American cause. Samuel and Betty spent much of their time refitting and repairing old muskets and match-locks.

After the Battle of Concord and Lexington, the British soldiers had left six brass cannons behind. Betty, who had acted as a nurse after the battles, saw the cannons and told Samuel about them. The British had spiked the guns when they abandoned them, but Samuel and Betty knew they could repair them. Soon the cannons were repaired and presented to the American Army. Betsy then began preparing ammunition for the army.

Sources: 1.*The Pioneer Mothers of America* by Harry Clinton Green and Mary Wolcott Green, pages 208-217.

****

Anne Kennedy Hamilton

Anne was born on June 11, 1761 in South Carolina, and she died on March 24, 1836 in Pickens County, South Carolina. She married Thomas Hamilton on December 18, 1782, and they had twelve children.

In 1780 Tories went to the Kennedy home looking for Anne's father and brothers. Her cousin, who had been wounded in a recent battle, was the only man they found. They felt that he would soon die from his wounds, so they decided not to kill him. As in most cases the Tories plundered the house. They took jewelry, the rings off the fingers of the ladies, bedclothes, and tore up featherbeds.

Anne's mother tried to save the last blanket by sitting on it, but one of the Tories pushed her off and took it. Anne lost her temper and grabbed the man by the arm, and she actually kicked him out the door. The Tory turned around to shoot her but his Captain intervened and prevented it. One Tory picked a fire brand from the hearth and said he would burn the house the house down. Anne, still angry, threw him out of the house. The Captain told the men the house would not be burned down. This enraged the man that had been thrown out, so he threw the firebrand at Anne, which struck her on the hand breaking some bones. For the rest of her life her hand was crippled by this action.

When the Tories left, the women feared they might return and kill the wounded cousin so they moved him out into the woods for safety. There Anne nursed him back to health, and he recovered after a few weeks. Soon after this the women in the neighborhood grew annoyed by the raiding Tories. They wrote a note to the American General Morgan who was stationed near the area. They requested that the General send some men to take care of the Tories. Anne was the only person that stepped forward to carry the letter nearly sixty miles to the General. She hid the note in her stocking and pinned a sunbonnet on her head and rode off.

In January of 1781 Anne watched a large group of British soldiers march by her home. She took mental notes of the size of the force and their equipment, and she rode to General Morgan with the information. This information helped the Americans to defeat the British at The Battle of Cowpens on January 17, 1781.

Sources: 1. Tombstone. 2. Sons of the American Revolution Application. 3. Anderson County Museum Advisory Committee selections for the Hall of Fame Class in 2015. 4. The Carolina Herald and Newsletter Pinckneyville Community of Camden District.

****

Nancy Hart

Nancy Hart or Aunt Nancy, as she was called by the "Liberty Boys", was a rough frontier woman. She was described as about six feet tall with red hair, a smallpox scarred face, and very strong. She was also a little cross-eyed and not exactly a thing of beauty. What she lacked in looks, she made up in courage and spirit.

Tories feared and hated her, because her husband was the captain of a patriot militia company. She served as a spy and kept her husband informed of the movements of the Tories. Many of the women and children had moved from the area to safety. Nancy refused to leave her home and remained there with her six boys and two girls.

One night she was boiling a pot of lye soap in the big fireplace in her cabin. She suddenly noticed a pair of eyes peering at her in a crack between the logs of the cabin. She pretended not to notice the prowler and continued to stir her pot. She threw a ladleful of the boiling soap into the prying eyes of the intruder who yelled with pain. She went outside and tied up the man, and in the morning she marched him to the patriot camp about four miles away. She walked carrying her rifle behind the man with his hands tied and turned him over to General Clarke.

On another occasion she met a Tory on her property, and after talking to him for a while she seized his gun. There was a struggle for the weapon but her strength and size won the fight. She marched the man a mile and a half to a patriot fort and turned over her prisoner of war.

One day in 1779 five or six British soldiers and Tories came to her house and demanded information about the location of a certain patriot leader. A short time earlier the patriot had been at her cabin, and Nancy had helped him escape. She told the Tories that the accusation was true. The men then demanded that she prepare food for them. She refused saying that she never fed traitors and King's men if she could help it. The men became angry and began to kill a couple of her animals. She asked the men to spare her prized turkey saying, *"The old gobbler out there in the yard is all I have left."*

The leader of the men went into the yard and shot her turkey. He handed the dead bird to Nancy and demanded that she cook it for them. This would prove to be a costly mistake for the men. Nancy, with the help of several of her children began preparing food for the hated Tories.

Nancy sent her thirteen year old daughter, Sukey, supposedly out to the spring for water, but she told the girl to blow a prearranged signal on a horn to alert the neighbors. Nancy then began to jest with the men and even shared some of the liquor the men had.

Meanwhile, the men had stacked their rifles in a corner of the cabin and were drinking wine and corn liquor and relaxing by the fire. Since the men were ignoring her, she began to pass their rifles out through a hole in the cabin wall to her daughter outside. One of the men saw her and began to approach her, so she pointed a rifle toward him and ordered him to stop.

Either the man did not think she would shoot or, as some people told the story, since she was cross-eyed, the man wasn't sure if she was looking at him or not. Regardless of the reason he advanced toward her, and she shot him dead. Another man made a move toward her, and she grabbed another rifle and shot and wounded him. Nancy grabbed another rifle, and blocking the doorway she ordered the men to surrender. One of the men said, *"Yes we will surrender, let's shake hands on the strength of it."* Now Nancy was guilty of not being attractive, but not guilty of being stupid. She pointed the rifle at the men and told them to sit down.

Nancy Hart from *Stories of Georgia* by Joel Chandler Harris. American Book Company, 1896.

She held off the remaining men until her husband and neighbors arrived to help. Her husband wanted to shoot the men, but Nancy, who was probably still angry about her turkey, insisted that the men hang. The remaining Tories were taken out to a tree and hung. Years later many people believed this story to just be an old folk tale. Nancy and her husband had moved off and the cabin was falling apart. In 1912 workmen were digging near the site of the old cabin and unearthed a row of six skeletons in tattered British uniforms laying side by side.

Sources: 1. *Nancy Hart, Georgia Heroine of the Revolution: The Story of the Growth of a Tradition* by E. Merton Coulter, Georgia Historical Quarterly 39, June 1955. 2. *Nancy Hart: Too Good Not to Tell Again in Georgia Women: Their Lives and Times* by John Thomas Scott, Vol. 1. 3. *Women Patriots of the American Revolution a Biographical Dictionary* by Charles E. Claghorn. 4. *Revolutionary Reader, Reminiscences and Indian Legends* compiled by Sophie Lee Foster, D.A.R. of Georgia, 1913, pages 252-255. 5. *Giant Days or the Life and Times of William H. Crawford* by J.E.D. Shipp, 1908, pages 17-21.

****

Molly Ludwig Hays ("Molly Pitcher")

Molly Pitcher at the Battle of Monmouth. Engraving by J.C. Armytage from painting by Alonzo Chappel. National Archives

Molly was born October 13, 1754 near Trenton, New Jersey, and she died January 22, 1832 in Pennsylvania. She married John Hays on July 24, 1769. Her husband served in the 7th Pennsylvania Regiment which was commanded by Colonel William Irvine. Molly served as a maid to the Colonel, and he took her along on his expeditions.

The Battle of Monmouth was the last major engagement fought in the northern theater of the war. The British holed up in New York would later shift their attention to the southern colonies. This battle is often remembered for the legend of "Molly Pitcher." During the battle temperatures on the field were over 100 degrees. William Hayes was an artilleryman and was at the battle.

During the battle Molly brought water to the soldiers from a spring that she found. Her husband either was wounded or dropped from heat exhaustion, so Molly took his place at the cannon. Cannons needed a constant supply of water to cool down the hot barrels and soak the sponge on the end of the ramrod used to clean out the barrels. Molly took her husband's place and continued to swab and load the cannon.

During the battle a British musket ball passed between her legs and tore off the bottom of her petticoat. She made a quick remark to the effect of *"Well if that had been higher it could have been worse."* When the battle had ended, General Washington wanted to know who the woman was that he had seen loading the cannon. He issued a warrant making her a noncommissioned officer. Years later she liked using the nickname *"Sergeant Molly."* It is believed that Molly Pitcher got her last name, when during the battle the soldiers that needed water would cry out, *"Molly—pitcher!"*

In her later years she was often seen in the streets of her town wearing a striped skirt, wool stockings, and a ruffled cap. The people in town liked her even though they said she *"often cursed like a soldier."* In 1822 Pennsylvania awarded her an annual pension of $40 for her service.

"Moll Pitcher she stood by her gun,
And rammed the charges home, sir,
And thus on Monmouth's bloody field,
A sergeant did become sir."

Sources: 1. *They Called Her Molly Pitcher* by Anne Rockwell. 2. *A Short History of Molly Pitcher, the Heroine of the Battle of Monmouth* by John B. Landis. 3. *A Treasury of Heroes and Heroines: A Record of High Endeavor and Strange Adventure* by Clayton Edwards, 1920, pages 196-200. 4. *Revolutionary Reader, Reminiscences and Indian Legends* complied by Sophie Lee Foster, D.A.R., 1913, page 195.

****

Heroic Women at the Battles of Lexington and Concord

Hannah Barron: When the British marched into Concord on April 19, 1775 they began to search the homes and buildings for rebel supplies. At a local tavern some of the soldiers went upstairs to open and search the rooms. In one room they found a young servant girl, Hannah Barnes, blocking the door. She said the room and the chest inside were hers and for them to go away. The soldiers obeyed her command. Inside her room in the chest was the money of the Provincial treasury.

Abigail Wright: She was the wife of the Concord Tavern proprietor and was said to have hidden the Church communion silver in soap barrels to avoid their being stolen. The same tale is attributed to Mrs. Jeremiah Robinson, who supposedly gathered the silver, hid it in her basement soap barrels, and barricaded her door against British intrusion.

Rebecca Barrett: She was the wife of Concord's militia colonel. A group of British troops, consisting of four companies under Captain Lawrence Parsons, began to march to Colonel James Barrett's farm about two miles away. Intelligence gathered by the spy Ensign De Bernicre indicated there was military equipment stored there. According to the spy they would find gunpowder, weapons, and two cannons.

Fortunately, most of the supplies had earlier been concealed in a field. Barrett's sons had tilled the fields and buried some of the arms in the furrows of the field. Musket balls were taken to the attic and placed in barrels and then covered with feathers.

At the Barrett house the British soldiers ransacked the house and demanded food from Mrs. Barrett. She prepared food and drink for them which they paid for. At first she refused payment and said it was her Christian duty to feed her enemies. They insisted and threw the money in her lap. She accepted the money saying, *"This is the price of blood."* Captain Parsons marched back to the North Bridge outside of Concord empty-handed of rebel supplies.

Meliscent Barrett: She was the 15 year old granddaughter of James and Rebecca. She had learned from a British officer how to roll powder cartridges. On the night of April 18th she supervised young women of Concord in preparing these items, which were most likely used against the Regulars at North Bridge.

****

Hannah Israel

HANNAH ERWIN ISRAEL SAVING THE CATTLE.   (Page 480)

Hannah's maiden name was Erwin, and her ancestors were Quakers who came to this country with William Penn. She was born in Wilmington, Delaware and first met her husband on a sloop sailing from Philadelphia to New Castle. Israel saw a pretty girl of seventeen on deck with blue eyes, dark hair, and very finely dressed. On these voyages the passengers furnished themselves with provisions. Hannah was sharing her food with others and offered him a portion of her food. It was love at first sight for the pair.

Illustration from "The Story of a Great Nation: Or, Our Country's Achievements, Military, Naval, Political and Civil", by John Gilmary Shea, published 1886.

After Israel saw his mother, he visited Hannah in Wilmington. After a respectable courtship he proposed marriage and the proposal was accepted. The couple raised a family on a farm near New Castle. Israel was an ardent supporter of the American cause for freedom. He once remarked that, *"I would sooner drive my cattle as a present to George Washington, than receive thousands of dollars in British gold for them."*

One day the British arrived to take the cattle from the farm. Hannah saw the troops land and march toward their farm. Her husband was not home so she got an eight year old boy to help her round up the cattle and save them from the British.

The British soldiers saw what she was doing and called out to her to stop or be shot. *"Fire away!"* she yelled back at the soldiers. They began firing, and with balls flying all over the cattle began to run in every direction. Hannah and the boy were able to round up the cattle, while the balls continued to fly around her. The young boy fell to the ground in fear and Hannah lifted him up and over the fence. She then drove the cattle by herself into the barnyard. The British impressed by her courage and not wishing to invade her property any further returned to their ship.

Hannah and her husband had thirteen children. Hannah died near Philadelphia at the age of fifty-six.

Sources: 1. *Daughters of America on Women of the Century*, by Phebe A. Hannaford, page 58. 2. *Women of the Revolution Vol. 1* by Elizabeth Ellet, pages 155-169.

****

Mammy Kate

On February 14, 1779 Stephen Heard was one of the Americans captured by the hated Tories. The captured men were taken to Fort Cornwallis in Augusta, Georgia and imprisoned. When Heard's slave Mammy Kate learned that her master was in prison, she mounted his horse Lightfoot, took another horse, and rode about 50 miles to the prison.

She left the horse in a safe place outside of town and devised a plan to free Stephen. She got a clothes basket and went to the fort offering to do washing for the British officers. She soon gained the trust of the officers due to her good work. On one visit she asked if she could wash Heard's clothes. At first the officers declined saying that he was going to hang soon. She replied, *"Let him hang in clean clothes."*

They finally agreed, so Kate would visit Heard twice a week and take and return his clothing in a basket that she carried on top of her head. She also would sneak cake into Heard's cell by putting it between her breasts. She later told her children, *"I had to put dat bread in my bosom to get it to master. But I always took it out 'fore I got dar, 'cause he was might perticler."*

One evening as the sun was going down, she left Heard's cell with his clothes in the basket on top of her head. As she passed by the guards, it would be the last time they would ever see her. In the basket, covered by some clothes was Heard. Luckily, Heard was a small man, and Kate was described *"as the biggest and tallest black woman"* local people had ever seen.

As soon as she was out of sight of the guards, she let Heard out and the two ran to where the horses were hidden. On the ride back a grateful Heard told her he was going to set her free for saving his life. She told him he could set her free, but she would never set him free. She was comfortable living on the plantation owned by Heard. Heard, who later became governor of Georgia, did set her free, gave her a small tract of land, and a four-roomed home that she lived in until her death.

Sources: 1. *Grandmother Stories from the Land of Used-to-Be* by Howard Meriwether Lovett. 2. *History of Elbert County, Georgia 1790-1935* by John H. McIntosh. 3. Kate Book. Com, a Website for Kates, by Kates, and About Kates.

****

Mary Knight

Mary was the sister of General Warrel, and she aided in relieving the sufferings of the American troops at Valley Forge. She cooked and carried provisions to them during the cold, hard winter. At times she passed the British outposts disguised as a market-woman.

The British placed a price on the head of her brother, and she concealed him for three days in a cider hogshead (cider cask). Her house was searched on four different occasions by the British looking for her brother. She passed the General food through the bunghole of the hogshead.

Sources: 1. *Daughters of America on Women of the Century*, by Phebe A. Hannaford, page 63. 2. Daughters of the American Revolution Magazine, Vol. 5 July to December, 1895.

****

Anna Maria Lane

Anna was born c. 1755, and she died on June 13, 1810. Anna achieved fame by being Virginia's only female soldier in the Revolutionary War. She went with her husband when he joined the Continental Army in 1776.

Many women like Anna served in the Revolutionary War. Most were camp followers who accompanied their husbands or family members. Some of these women sought adventure or were in search of a living. Most were involved in cooking, nursing, or doing wash.

However, Anna dressed as a man performed the duties of a soldier. Together she and her husband fought in several early battles. At the Battle of Germantown fought on October 4, 1777, Anna received a serious leg wound that left her lame for the rest of her life. Before the battle, Washington issued an order that forbid women in camp to follow their men into battle. Some historians believe that the severity of Anna's leg wound was due to the fact she did not seek treatment for the wound for fear of being discovered.

In 1801 Anna worked as a nurse in a military hospital and was paid a small amount for the work. By 1804 she was too feeble to work, and she applied to the state for a pension. In 1808 she received a pension of $100 a year from the State of Virginia for her service. It was read into the state record on January 28, 1808, *".....Anna Maria Lane is also very infirm, having been disable by a severe wound, which she received WHILE FIGHTING AS A COMMON SOLDIER, in one of our Revolutionary battles, from which she never has recovered, and perhaps never will recover."*

Sources: 1. *Battle Cries and Lullabies* by Linda Grant DePauw. 2. *Virginia Soldiers of 1776*, pages 1277-8. 3. *Anna Maria Lane: An Uncommon Soldier of the American Revolution* by Sandra Treadway, Virginia Cavalcade 37, no. 3, 1988, pages 134-143. 4. Anna Marie Lane marker in Richmond, Virginia.

****

Dicey Langston

Dicey Langston was born on May 14, 1766 in Laurens County, South Carolina, and she died on May 23, 1837 in Greenville County, South Carolina. She married Thomas Springfield on January 9, 1783.

By the time Dicey was fifteen she was as good a shot and horsewoman as anyone in the county. During the war her brothers and a small group of patriots made a camp several miles from the Langston farm. The area was a hotbed of Tory activity, and persons that supported the patriots had to be careful. Since many of the neighbors and some of the relatives of Dicey were loyal to the Tories, it was easy for her to gather information on Tory activity when she went for visits.

The Tories began to wonder why so much information about their movements were getting to the rebels. The Tories began to suspect that Solomon Langston was involved with spying and perhaps his daughter as well. One time they paid Solomon a visit, and they threatened him and said that if Dicey was involved in spying they would hold him accountable for her actions.

Solomon knew that she had been giving information to her brother's camp and demanded that she stop. She agreed, but after a brief period of time she continued with her spying.

In 1781 she heard that a ruthless gang of Tories called the Bloody Scouts, and led by the infamous Bloody Bill Cunningham, was in the area. The gang had burned homes and massacred rebels and their supporters during the past year. Dicey learned that the gang was planning to raid a village known as Little Eden, which was also near her brother's camp. She knew that she had to warn her brother.

She decided that the safest way to travel was by foot and at night. She left late one night and stayed off the roads keeping to the fields and woods. She came upon a creek that had become swollen by the spring rains. As she crossed the creek she lost her footing, and the swift cold water carried her downstream trying to pull her under. She finally pulled herself up on the river bank and laid there to regain her strength. She was exhausted and cold, but she knew that she had to continue to her brother's camp.

She finally made it to her brother's camp and warned them of the imminent attack. The men had just returned from an expedition and, like Dicey, were also cold and tired. She built a fire and made them hoecakes to eat. The men took the food and left to warn the people in the area of the Tory attack. When the Bloody Scouts arrived the next morning, they found the camp deserted and the people in the area had vanished. Dicey's act of courage had saved many lives.

After Dicey gave the soldiers food she returned home, and she once again went through fields, woods, and crossed cold streams. Dicey made it back home in time to dry off and prepare breakfast for her father. As Solomon ate she did not mention what had transpired during the night. The Bloody Scouts were angry that their mission had failed and, although they could not prove it, they suspected that Solomon Langston was behind it.

Later, they paid a visit to the Langston home with the intent of killing Solomon and looting the house. When the Tories arrived at the Langston home they entered and pointed a gun at Solomon. Before they could fire, Dicey quickly jumped between her father and the man pointing the pistol. She told them that they would have to kill her first. One of the Tories was so impressed with the young girl's courage, that he stopped the man from discharging his pistol and made the men leave.

Dicey Langston protecting her father from Tories. Library of Congress.

This would not be the last time that Dicey would stand up to the threats of the Tories. On one occasion she was returning from meeting some rebel friends in the Spartanburg area, when she was stopped by a group of Tories. They demanded to know where she had been and the names of the people, or she would die in her tracks. Dicey replied, *"Shoot me if you dare! I will not tell you."* She then removed a handkerchief that covered her neck and the top of her chest, as if to offer a place to be shot. The man was about to fire, when another man stopped him and saved Dicey's life.

On another occasion she was home alone when several Tories began banging on her door demanding entrance. She answered back in a stern voice that they should leave at once. The men began talking among themselves trying to decide what to do. Finally, they gave up and left.

Her brother James, a rebel leader, had left a rifle in her care and told her to keep it until he sent for it. One day a group of men showed up at the Langston home asking for the rifle. She retrieved the rifle, and as she entered back into the room where the men were waiting she remembered that her brother said that if anyone came to claim the rifle they should give a countersign to prove that they were patriots. Dicey did not recognize these men and feared they might be Tories, so she asked for the countersign. One of the men told her it was a little late to be making conditions since the rifle and she were clearly in their possession. Dicey cocked the rifle and pointed it at the man and said, *"If the gun is in your possession, take charge of here!"* The man could tell by her look and the tone of her voice that she meant business. He quickly gave the countersign, and they all had a good laugh. One of the men remarked to Dicey that she was certainly worthy to be called the sister of James Langston.

Sources: 1. *Women Patriots of the American Revolution: a Biographical Dictionary* by Charles E. Claghorn. 2. *The Women of the American Revolution* by Elizabeth F. Ellet, 3rd edition, 1849. 3. *Women in the American Revolution* by Paul Engle.

****

Mrs. Latham

Fort Griswold was captured on September 6, 1781 by the British led by the American traitor Benedict Arnold. Captain William Latham was wounded in the thigh and he was taken to New York along with his ten year old son William and with the other prisoners. His son William was placed under guard with the other prisoners.

As the town of New London was being looted and burned by the British, the wife of Captain Latham and her daughter Mary made their way to the fort to look for her husband and son. She first went to Ebenezer Avery's house, which was being used as a hospital. At the door the sentry held out his rifle to prevent them from entering. Unafraid, Mrs. Latham pushed his rifle aside and went into the house. Once inside she saw wounded friends and neighbors but did not find her family. She kept looking all night, and in the morning she went to the headquarters' of Benedict Arnold and asked about her son.

She found young William sitting with the other prisoners paralyzed with terror and in great distress. It was the 7th of September, and the boy had eaten no food since the night of the 5th. He was fatigued from the heat and the fear of all he had seen in the battle. He had a piece of bread in his hand but had not eaten it for fear that the British had poisoned it.

Mrs. Latham knew Benedict Arnold well since he was a native of Norwich. She said to him, *"Benedict Arnold, I come for my child. Not to ask for him but demand him of you." "Take him,"* replied Arnold. *"Take him, and don't you bring him up a damned rebel." "I shall take him,"* she said, *"and teach him to despise the name of a traitor."* All members of the Latham family survived the war.

Sources: 1. *Genealogical Notes of the Williams and Gallup Families* by Charles F. Williams, 1897. 2. The Connecticut Magazine, Vol. 9 William Farrand Felch, George Atwell, H. Phelps Arms, and Francis Treelyan Miller, 1905.

****

Agnes Dickinson Lee

Agnes was born in 1745 and died in 1830. She married Samuel Lee in 1763, and when the war started their home became a center of patriotic activities in Guilford, Connecticut. The couple collected all types of pewter and lead that could be used to melt down and make bullets. The house was filled with confiscated goods, laces, silks, thread, and buttons strung and hung behind the four-posted bed in the west bedroom. These items were almost impossible to obtain.

The Tories targeted her house much of the time. One time when they rode up she was working with some of the items and she threw the ribbons, lace, and buttons into the cooking pot over the fire successfully fooling the Tories.

In 1755 a British Man of War had left a small cannon at the wharf in Guilford. The home guard took the cannon and mounted it near a willow tree next to the Lee's house. The cannon was to be used to alarm the back country. Sometimes people were warned if the cannon was going to be used. Once they were warned, they would open all their windows to prevent the breaking of glass.

In 1781 the British landed at nearby Leet's Island, and unfortunately there were no men around the house to fire the cannon. Agnes went out to fire the cannon, or as she later said, *"went out and blazed away."* The militia responded to the warning of the cannon and repulsed the British landing party.

One night when her husband was out of town, he had his brother Levi stay at the house to protect his family. Levi had left the house for a short period of time during the evening, and the Tories happened to show up. They knocked at the front door and Agnes listening inside could hear their voices and knew that the Tories were outside.

"Who's there?" she asked. *"A friend,"* was the reply *"Yes, friends to King George and the traitors,"* Agnes replied, refusing to open the door.

As the Tories tried to kick the door in, Agnes pushed her three young daughters into her bedroom and locked them in. As the Tories came in Agnes held a candle high in the darkened room so that she could see their faces. They blew it out and she promptly relit it. The Tories then advanced to the bedroom door where the young girls were locked in. Agnes told them her children were in there and no one would enter except over her dead body. As the Tories hesitated Levi returned with two muskets in his hands. Agnes cried out, *"Shoot, Levi! I can load as fast as you can shoot."* Levi fired and as the Tories ran out of the house he continued to fire as fast as Agnes could load. The next morning Agnes noticed that in the snow outside of her house there were patches of blood. She later learned that the town doctor had treated a man with "rheumatism" in his elbow.

For a period of time barrels of gunpowder were stored in their attic room. Because of the summer heat the window was left open. A thundershower hit the area, and lighting struck the Lee's barn causing a fire. Sparks began to swirl in the area and were being blown into the open attic window. One of the powder barrels was left uncovered. Agnes rushed upstairs to close the window, and later said she never expected to come down those stairs alive. One of the daughters of Agnes told her grandchildren many years later how her mother ran up the stairs as calmly as though she was going to make the bed. While sparks were flying in her face she put the window down. The daughter added, *"She always did her duty in just that calm way."*

The local Tories suspected that rebel provisions were in the barn, because after the storm one of them remarked, *"We meant to have burned that barn, but the Almighty got ahead of us."*

Even after the war the Tories were still hateful to the patriots. When the oldest daughter of Agnes, Rebecca, was married, some Tory guest snipped pieces out of the back of her wedding gown during a party. When the couple left to go to their house on east Creek, they found ropes stretched across the road to trip the horses.

Henry B. Griswold, the great grandson of Agnes, described her as a little woman, a white kerchief about her throat, and knitting as she sat erect in her straight-back chair. A woman of dignity and charm and a great-grandmother who told delightful stories.

Sources: 1. *The Seward's of Guilford, Connecticut and the Experiences of one of them from 1848 to 1944* by Samuel Lee Seward, pages 6-9. 2. *Yester-Years of Guilford* by Mary Hoadley Griswold, 1938, pages 121-127.

****

Jeannette Leman

Jeannette Leman was born in 1768 in Ireland, and she died on October 8, 1856 in South Carolina. She married William Walker. At the age of twelve she carried secret dispatches to General Thomas Sumter in South Carolina. On one occasion she passed through a camp of Tories with a dispatch concealed in the heel of her stocking, where she had purposely knit a double heel.

Sources: 1. Tombstone 2. D.A.R. Lineage Book, Vol. 47.

****

Sybil Ludington

Sybil Ludington was born on April 5, 1761 in Fredericksburg, New York, and she died on February 26, 1839 in Patterson, New York. She married Edmond Ogden in 1784.

Sybil's father Henry Ludington was a patriot, and in 1776 he was appointed a Colonel in the 7th Dutchess County Militia. The area his regiment guarded was important, because it was the most direct route the British would take to and from Connecticut and the coast on Long Island Sound. The regiment also prevented Tories from obtaining supplies for the British.

Since Henry was a wanted man, sixteen year old Sybil felt obligated to guard and protect him from any dangers that threatened him. One night Ichabod Prosser, a hated Tory, and his men surrounded the Ludington house in hopes of capturing or killing Samuel. Sybil enlisted the help of her oldest sister to fool the Tories.

The two girls were guarding the house with their weapons ready to fire. When the Tories were spotted the girls sounded the alarm. Immediately, candles were lit in every room and the girls, along with several other family members, began marching back and forth in front of the windows. It appeared to the Tories hiding outside that the house was heavily guarded, so they marched on to the next town.

A message was sent to Colonel Ludington at his home on April 26, 1777. The message warned that the British were a few miles away in Danbury, Connecticut. They had uncovered American military stores and then began burning and looting the town. Unfortunately, Colonel Ludington's 400 militia men were on furlough and were scattered around the county. It would take a rider all night to alert the men to the British threat.

Sybil told her father she would make the ride, and over his objections she began to prepare for the ride. Around nine at night she began the forty mile ride that would take her to the towns of Carmel, Mahopac, Kent Cliffs, and Farmers Mills. Before she left, her father gave her a large thick stick to bang on the doors of the home to wake the sleeping men. He warned her to be on the lookout for Tory outlaws that roamed the area.

Off she rode to alert the countryside. Each home she came to she would bang on the door with the stick until a candle inside was lit. Then she would yell, *"The British are burning Danbury! Muster at Ludington's Mill."* This same scene was created all night until she returned home the next morning. Once during the night she even had to fight off an outlaw.

Statue of Sybil Ludington on Gleneida Avenue in Carmel, New York by Anna Hyatt Huntington.

By the time she got back to the mill yard it was swarming with militiamen, and later the militia caught up with the British and beat them back. The British boarded their ships and sailed away. They never attempted a similar raid.

Sources: 1. *Sybil Ludington The Call to Arms* by V.T. Dacquino. 2. *Danbury's Burning: The Story of Sybil Ludington's Ride* by Anne Grant.

****

Lydia Mackey

In 1781 South Carolina was overrun with British troops and their Tory allies. Charles Mackey was a patriot, and he led a band of men who fought with General Francis Marion. Charles was noted for being hard-headed, impulsive, and prone to taking unnecessary risks. His wife Lydia Mackey was the opposite, being a woman of good common sense, a clear head, and sound judgement.

The Mackey home was about two miles from the camp of British Lt. Colonel Tarleton. He was well known as a vicious, cruel, and hateful officer. Because of the close proximity of the British camp, Charles knew it would be extremely dangerous for him to visit his home. But being an impulsive person, he left his camp and went home for a visit. During his visit he would go out at times to the British camp to gather information.

He would spend most of his days in a nearby swamp and visit his home at night. He had a watch dog that would bark loudly whenever anyone approached the farm. One evening while home, the dog failed to sound an alarm when Tory riders approached. When they approached the house they yelled out, *"Hallo."* Mrs. Mackey jumped from her bed and looked out her second story window to see six armed men who were strangers.

She asked what they wanted and they said, *"Is Charlie Mackey at home?"* She replied that he was not, and while this conversation was taking place Charles was attempting to escape the house. He was about to raise a loose plank in the floor, crawl under the house to the back, and then make his way through the orchard to the swamp. He had successfully used this escape route on several occasions.

The riders told Mrs. Mackey that there was a big fight yesterday between General Marion and the British, and that the British were defeated. They said they had been sent with orders to join General Marion at Lansford and to attack Tarleton. They continued by saying, *"We do not know the way to Lansford, and have come to get Charlie to show us the way."*

The cautious Mrs. Mackey said she was sorry that her husband was not home to ride with them. Charles, hearing all of this and being impulsive, came out of the house and ran to the men shouting hurrahs for General Marion and vowing death to the British. The leader of the riders replied calmly, *"Well, Charlie, old fellow, we have set many traps for you, but never baited them right until now. You are our prisoner."* They bound him and rode off toward the camp of Tarleton. Once there he was tried and sentenced to death as a spy.

The next morning Mrs. Mackey figured that her husband would be taken to Tarleton's camp, so she gathered some fruit and eggs and rode to the camp. Once in the camp she met a young officer who told her that Colonel Tarleton was on parade and for her to take a seat. He asked her if she brought the eggs and fruit to sell. Lydia Mackey told the officer that she brought the food as a way to get to see Colonel Tarleton. She explained to the man that her husband was captured and wished to get him released, if he were still alive.

Again, she was told that the Colonel was on parade and would not return for at least two hours. Lydia, who could be rather charming, appealed to the softer side of the officer, who began to feel sorry for the woman. He said that he would prepare the papers for the release of her husband, and all Tarleton would have to do is sign the document. The officer, knowing that his Colonel was not noted for being understanding toward the desires of the Americans, told her that the Colonel probably would not sign it.

Around noon Colonel Tarleton, tall, handsome, and clean shaven rode up and entered his tent. The sympathetic officer told Lydia that the Colonel would have to dine first, before he could present the paper to him for a signature. Soon the Colonel came out of his tent and started to mount his horse. Lydia stepped forward and explained to him the purpose of her visit. The Colonel said he was in a hurry and could not help her at this time. Lydia explained that her husband had been condemned to death, and only the Colonel had the power to save him.

Tarleton brushed the woman off by saying, *"When I get back later in the day I'll look into it."* He then placed his foot in the stirrup and sprang up to mount his horse. Before he could throw his leg over, Lydia grabbed his coat and pulled him down. He turned to her in a fit of anger and said he would look into it when he returned. Again, he attempted to mount, and once more Lydia pulled him down begging him to spare her husband.

British Lt. Colonel Tarleton   National Archives

Tarleton was quite angry, for he had killed people for less than what this woman was doing. He said to her, *"Do you know what you are doing? I will attend to this at my convenience and not sooner."* He then turned to try to mount for the third time, and for the third time Lydia pulled him down.

This time she held the scabbard of his sword and fell to her knees. She cried out, *"Draw your sword and slay me, or give me the life of my husband, for I will never let you go until you kill me or sign this document,"* which she held up before his face.

Tarleton was trembling with rage, because no colonial had ever dared to treat him this way. He called out to his officer, *"Captain, where is this woman's husband?"* Tarleton was told the prisoner was in a nearby tent. *"Order him to be brought here,"* the Colonel demanded. Charley Mackey was brought before the red-faced Colonel who said, *"Sir, you have been convicted of bearing arms against His Majesty's government; worse, you have been convicted of being a spy.*

You have dared to enter my lines in disguise as a spy, and you cannot deny it, but for the sake of your wife I will give you a full pardon on condition that you will take an oath never again to bear arms against the King's government."

Now Charles Mackey was many things but dishonest was not among them. *"Sir,"* said Mackey, *"I cannot accept pardon on these terms. It must be unconditional or I must die."* Then poor Lydia also cried out, *"I, too, must die."* A shocked Tarleton turned to his Captain and paused before he spoke, *"Captain, for God's sake sign my name to this paper and let this woman go."* With that Tarleton was finally able to mount his horse, and he quickly rode off. This was probably the only nice gesture toward a colonial that Tarleton made during the entire Revolution.

Source: 1. *Revolutionary Reader, Reminiscences and Indian Legends* by Sophie Lee Foster, page, 88-93.

****

Elizabeth, Grace and Rachel Martin

Grace was born February 20, 1758 in South Carolina and died there in 1800. Rachel was born on June 19, 1763 in Virginia. The two women married the two older sons of Elizabeth and Abram Martin.

Elizabeth had nine children, and seven of the boys served in the American Army, but a younger son remained at home. She told her boys, *"Go, boys, fight for your country; never let your country be dishonored. If I were a man, I would go with you!"* One story tells that Elizabeth was visited by a British officer who told her that he had seen one of her sons die on the battlefield. Instead of seeing her cry, she replied, *"He could not have died in a nobler cause."*

Grace and Rachel lived with Elizabeth while their husbands went to war. One night news reached the Martin home that important dispatches were being sent to a British commander, and the rider would pass near the home. Grace and Rachel put on their husband's clothes, and each grabbed a rifle and walked down to the bend in the road where the courier would pass.

Soon horsemen, the courier, and two British soldiers were seen riding toward them. The two women sprang from the shadows and pointed the rifles at the trio. With a loud voice they called out, *"Surrender! You are my prisoners."*

The three riders threw down their weapons and gave the dispatches to the two disguised women. The three men were released, and Grace and Rachel slipped off into the darkness. The women took a shortcut through the woods, and when they arrived home they sent the dispatches by messenger to General Greene.

Within the hour the three British riders stopped at the Martin house and asked for a night's lodging. Elizabeth, Rachel, and Grace prepared food for the men and asked, *"Were you not sent with dispatches to British headquarters?"* The men told of being held up by two rebel boys and having their papers taken. One of the men added, *"The first I knew, one of those long rifles the rebels know so well how to handle, was in my face. There was no time to use our arms."*

It must have been very difficult for the three women to maintain their composure and not break out laughing. The three British soldiers never learned that they slept under the same roof as the "men" who had taken them prisoners.

Illustration from "The Story of a Great Nation: Or, Our Country's Achievements, Military, Naval, Political and Civil", by John Gilmary Shea, published 1886.

Sources: 1. *Encyclopedia of American Women at War: from the Home Front to the Battlefields* edited by Lisa Tendrich Frank, pages 374-375. 2. *Women Soldiers, Spies, and Patriots of the American Revolution* by Martha Kneib, pages 62-66. 3. *Grandmother Stories from the Land of Used-to-Be* by Howard Meriwether Lovett, 1913, pages 77-78. 4. *Revolutionary Reader, Reminiscences and Indian Legends* complied by Sophie Lee Foster, D.A.R., 1913, page 111.

****

Mary McClure

The Skirmish at Williamson's Plantation was a small but great victory for the Americans. The victory gave the South Carolina back country a boost. The frontier militia, a band of farmers, had defeated the feared British soldiers. After the skirmish many local men wanted to join the militia. The victory might not have been possible without the help of a young girl and a slave.

In June of 1780 the British officer, who commanded a British Provincial Regiment, ordered Captain Christian Huck to take a command of men to the area and find the rebel leaders, in order to persuade other locals to join the British side. He marched into one district, gathered all the men together, with most being old, and proclaimed, *"even if the rebels were as thick as trees, and Jesus Christ would come down and lead them, I would still defeat them."*

After making his boast, Captain Huck confiscated all the men's horses. The theft and the tirade did not make many friends with the local people. He was given the nickname, *"the swearing captain."*

On July 11, 1780 Captain Huck, with his four hundred British cavalry, arrived at the home of colonial Colonel William Bratton and asked his wife where her husband was. She replied that the Colonel was with the American Colonel Sumter. Captain Huck told her that if her husband would join him, he would gain a commission. The Colonel's wife replied, *"I desire that he should remain in Colonel Sumter's command even if he lost his life."* One of the British soldiers attempted to kill her for those remarks but was stopped. Captain Huck left, however, not before he arrested three old men on trumped up charges.

Around this time a neighbor's younger sister, Mary McClure, and a slave named Watt provided the militia commander with some valuable intelligence on the movements of Captain Huck. The militiamen arrived in the vicinity that night and prepared to attack Captain Huck. The next day they attacked the British from three sides and completely destroyed the British regiment. The braggart, Captain Huck, was killed.

Sources: 1. Christian Huck quote from Memoirs of Maj. Joseph McLunkin. 2. *Publications of the Southern History Association Vol. 1* by Colyer Meriwether. 3. Pension Papers of James McCaw S18117. 4. *A Guide to the Battles of the American Revolution* by Savas and Dameron.

****

Behethland Moore

Behethland Moore was born on December 24, 1764 in Faugwier County, Virginia, and she died on December 2, 1853 at the home of her son in Edgefield, South Carolina.

Behethland had several encounters with the enemy soldiers at a young age. One time a small band of Tories was ransacking the Moore house and ordered a servant to bring them the horses in the barn. Behethland commanded the young servant not to obey the Tory order. The soldier grew angry and threatened to beat the servant if he did not obey the order. Again, Behethland told the boy to stay where he was. The Tory then raised his fist to strike the boy, and Behethland quickly got between the boy and the Tory and refused to move. The soldier lowered his fist and walked away.

On another occasion in 1780 a small skirmish took place near her home between Colonel Washington's cavalry and the Tory militia led by Lord Rawdon. After the fighting ended, several of the Tory militiamen entered Behethland's home in search of plunder. The only people inside the house were Behethland, two younger brothers, her mother, and a friend named Fanny Smith. Luckily, the family had been warned in advance that the Tories were in the area, so they hid their most valuable possessions.

A soldier searching upstairs found two barrels of apples, which he began to roll down the stairs to another soldier below. Behethland and her brother had spent the whole morning picking the apples and were not happy that their work would go to waste. The young teenager grew angry, and showing no fear she ordered the men to stop at once because the apples belonged to her. A Tory officer standing nearby was impressed with the young girl's courage and ordered the men to stop.

The officer told his men that they would have all the fruit they could eat in the morning, when they were at the rebel Wallace's camp. After the Tories had left, Behethland told her mother that she must get to the camp of Captain Wallace and warn them that the Tories were going to attack. The rebel camp was across the Saluda River a few miles upstream from the Moore home.

As the sun began to go down over the horizon, fifteen year old Behethland, a younger brother, and their friend Fanny got a canoe and began to paddle to the rebel camp. As they paddled each kept an eye toward shore hoping they would not spot any Tories. They paddled for miles, their bodies ached with pain, and their hands became raw from the constant paddling. Finally, they saw the flickering light from several campfires, and they knew they had reached their destination.

The trio delivered their message of warning to Captain Wallace and turned to leave. The Captain asked them to stay, eat, and rest. Behethland refused and told the Captain they needed to return home. The three children returned back to the Moore house just before daybreak, and they were totally exhausted from their all night journey. The next day when the Tories reached the American camp, they found it deserted.

Around noon the day Behethland returned home, a young rebel officer rode up to the Moore house and asked to speak to the girl that carried the message that saved the rebel soldiers. Word had spread through the ranks of her daring adventure, and he was sent to hear her story. The young Captain Butler was quite surprised when a beautiful girl introduced herself as the person he sought. Behethland was herself drawn to the handsome young officer in uniform, and she was eager to spend time with him telling her story.

For the next several years the young Captain found every excuse possible to visit the Moore farm to talk with Behethland. In 1784 Behethland and Captain William Butler were married. William later served in Congress for thirteen years, and during the War of 1812 he was made a Major General in command of the South Carolina forces at Camden.

Sources: 1. *Women Patriots of the American Revolution: a Biographical Dictionary* by Charles E. Claghorn. 2. *The Romance of the Revolution: Being True Stories of Adventure, Romantic Incidents, Hairbreadth Escapes, and Heroic Exploits of the Days of '76.* 3. *The Part Taken by Women in America History* by Mrs. John A. Logan, 1912, pages 142-3. 4. *The Women of the American Revolution Vol. II* by Elizabeth F. Ellet, 1900, pages 95-105.

****

Mary Murry

After the Battle of Brooklyn in August of 1776, General Washington's troops began to retreat. In September of the same year British General William Howe landed troops in Kip's Bay in order to trap the retreating Americans.

Mary Murry, a patriot, realized the Americans were within a mile from her home on Long Island, and that the British had twice the number of soldiers. If the British were not stopped, the Americans would be trapped and captured. As the British troops approached Mary's home, she asked the officers if they would like to stop and have cake and wine.

The British officers agreed, and Mary fed them while her daughters entertained them. Mary had a maid go upstairs and keep watch from the window to let her know when the American troops were safely withdrawn. By the time the meal was completed, the Americans had withdrawn to safety.

Legend portrays Mary as tempting the British officers with her charms. However, it should be noted that Mary was in her fifties and the mother of twelve children. A few historians doubt that the event even took place. The story of Mary was developed into two Broadway plays: *Dearest Enemy* in 1925, and *A Small War on Murray Hill* in 1957.

Sources: 1. *Revolutionary Women: In the War for American Independence* edited by Lincoln Diamant. 2. *Seventeen Seventy-Six* by David McCullough.

****

Mary Redmond

Mary was known around Philadelphia as "the little black-eyed rebel." She gained this nickname, because she was always ready to help in passing intelligence about the British to the Americans. Many times dispatches were sent by young boys who had the messages sewed into the back of their coats.

On one morning when the British seemed suspicious of one boy carrying the secret message, Mary decided to get the papers from him. Mary went to the market as usual and pretended to play a game with the boy. At one point she threw her shawl over the boy and managed to get the papers from him. She then turned the information over to her contact, who took the messages to the American army. When news came of the surrender of the British General Burgoyne, Mary went home to rejoice in private. Once inside her home, she put her head up the chimney and gave a shout for American General Gates.

Sources: 1. *Daughters of America on Women of the Century*, by Phebe A. Hannaford, page 58. 2. *Women of the Revolution Vol. 1*. By Elizabeth Ellet, pages 169-171.

****

Esther de Berdt Reed

Esther was born on October 22, 1746 in London, England, and she died on September 18, 1780 in Philadelphia, Pennsylvania. She married Joseph Reed in London on May 31, 1770. Joseph was born in New Jersey and had come to London to pursue a law degree. In October the couple came to the colonies, and they brought Esther's mother who had become bankrupt.

By 1774 Esther began to support the patriot cause. She was troubled by the way England treated the American colonists, and she soon began to speak out for independence. On November 2, 1774 she wrote a letter to her brother Dennis in London and mentioned the strained relations between the two countries. She also wrote of little hope that the two countries could resolve their differences. She wrote,

"The people of New England have not such expectations. They are prepared for the worst event, and they have such ideas of their injured

liberty, and so much enthusiasm in the cause, that I do not think that any power on earth could take it from them but with their lives."

Joseph was elected President of the Pennsylvania government in 1778, and the family moved to Philadelphia. Esther became more outspoken for independence, and in January of 1780 she contributed to a broadside published in Philadelphia called "The Sentiments of an American Woman." Her writings encouraged women to support the war and declared that women were the equals of men in patriotism by referring to women as "brave Americans." She urged women to *"render themselves more really useful"* to the public good.

She became aware of the terrible living conditions of the American troops, their ragged clothing, and lack of food. After her recovery from smallpox, she founded the Ladies' Association of Philadelphia. It was at the time the largest women's organization in America. They campaigned to raise funds to help the American soldiers.

The women hoped the gift of money would show how dedicated American women were to the cause of patriotism. Esther wrote to General Washington on July 4, 1780 that the women had raised more than $300,000 continental dollars. When converted to precious-metal coin, it was more than $7,500. Esther wanted to give the men gold or silver coins, beyond their normal pay.

The women shunned the traditional polite rules of behavior, which barred door to door asking for money. The women went about contacting every household in Philadelphia, giving them a copy of Reed's essay "The Sentiments of an American Woman", and then asking for money. They approached all levels of society, as the biographer for Mr. Reed wrote, *"All ranks of society seem to have joined in the liberal effort, from Phillis, the colored woman, with her humble seven shillings and six pence, to the Marchioness de La Fayette, who contributed one hundred guineas in specie."* La Fayette wrote a nice letter to Esther on June 25, 1780,

"Madam, In admiring the new resolution, in which the fair ones of Philadelphia have taken the lead, I am induced to feel for those American ladies, who being out of the Continent cannot participate in this patriotic measure. I know of one who, heartily wishing for a personal acquaintance with the ladies of America, would feel particularly happy to be admitted among them on the present occasion. Without presuming to break in upon the rules of your respected association, may I most numbly present myself as her ambassador to the confederate ladies, and solicit in her name that Mrs. President [Esther was called Mrs. President while her husband was President of the Pennsylvania government] *be pleased to accept of her offering. With the highest respect, I have the honor to be, Madam, your most obedient servant, La Fayette."*

Washington responded to Esther on July 14, 1780, *"If I am happy in having the concurrence of the Ladies, I would propose the purchasing of course Linen, to be made into Shirts, with the whole amount of their subscription. A Shirt extraordinary to the Soldier will be of more service, and do more to preserve his health than any other thing that could be procured him. This appears to me, to be the best mode for its application, and provided it is approved of by the Ladies."*

Privately, Washington was fearful that if the men received the extra money they would purchase liquor with it. The ladies approved the suggestion of Washington, and with the aid of volunteer seamstresses more than 2,200 shirts were made for the soldiers.

Sadly, Esther did not live to see the completion of her efforts. She died on September 18, 1780 at the age of thirty-four. Sarah Franklin Bache took over Esther's position and finished the project she had begun. After Esther's death, George Washington wrote to her husband that he regretted *"the loss of your amiable lady."*

Sources: 1. *The Sentiments of an American Woman* by John Dunlap. 2. *Women of the Revolution Vol. 1.* by Elizabeth Ellet, pages 37-56. 3. *Women Patriots of the American Revolution: A Biographical Dictionary* by Charles E. Claghorn, pages 160-161.

****

Molly "Mom" Rinker

Molly Rinker ran the Buck Tavern in Germantown during the Revolution. When the British occupied the town, they took over her tavern and made it their home. She had to serve them food and drink, which gave her ample opportunity to hear bits of information that would be of value to the American army.

As the British officers drank they talked freely about the plans of their army, and Molly was very willing to listen. The soldiers had banned male members from the dining area where they sat and talked. They were not concerned about Molly listening in, because she was just a woman and not bright enough to understand what they were talking about. She made sure that there were ample supplies of liquor in the room so that she would not have to leave and miss anything.

Molly had a very unique way of passing the valuable information to General Washington. Later in the evening Molly would write down what she heard on small strips of paper and wrap them around a tiny stone. She then wrapped yarn around the stone to conceal the paper. The next day she would go to a nearby creek and sit on a large rock on a cliff overlooking the water and the road.

She would spend the day knitting socks that she sent to the soldiers. This act in itself was illegal and could get her locked up by the British. When she saw one of her contacts riding toward the cliff, she would either lower the ball of yarn with the attached message or drop it from the cliff. The rider would retrieve the message and take it to General Washington.

Her contribution to the war effort paid off during the Battle of Germantown. General John Armstrong who led troops under General Washington praised Molly for saving many of his men. He said that without her information his troops would have been doomed. Although the Americans lost the battle, their army impressed the French so much that they decided to give the Americans more aid.

Sources: 1. *No Idle Hands: The Social History of American Knitting* by Anne MacDonald, page 37. 2. *Turncoats, Traitors, and Heroes* by John Bakeless, page 208. 3. *Spies, Patriots, and Traitors: American Intelligence in the Revolutionary War* by Nenneth A. Daigler, page 143. 4. *Encyclopedia of American Women at War: From the Home Front to the Battlefields, Vol 1.* By Lisa Tendrich Frank, page 471-72.

****

Sally Salter

The Battle of Tory Hole was fought on August 27, 1781 between the patriot militia of Bladen County and the Tory militia of Bladen County. The patriots were not sure of how many of the enemy they faced, so Sally Salter the young wife of a local man offered to enter the enemy's camp and find out.

73

She took a basket of eggs, took the ferry across Cape Fear River, and entered the camp of the Tories. She walked around the camp selling her eggs and making mental notes of what she saw. After acquiring what she needed, she went back across the river to report her findings.

Because the Tories had taken all the boats, that night the patriots crossed the river naked with their clothes tied in bundles on top of their heads. Once across they got dressed and at daybreak took the Tory camp by surprise. The outnumbered patriots began to shout out commands to fictitious units, and many of the men also yelled out, "Washington". The Tories thinking they were under attack by a large force panicked and ran. Many of the enemy ran into a deep ravine where they were easy to shoot at. This site became known as Tory Hole. Nineteen of the enemy were killed with no loss of patriot lives. Some Tory survivors of the battle reported that they were attacked by Washington's whole army.

Sources: 1. *Dictionary of North Carolina Biography: Vol. 5, P-S*, edited by William S. Powell. 2. *Historical Sketches of North Carolina from 1584 to 1851* by John H. Wheeler.

****

Sarah Hartwell Shattuck

Sarah, the wife of Job Shattuck, was born on March 19, 1738, and she died on May 5, 1798. A few days after the Battle of Lexington and Concord it was expected that the noted Tory, Leonard Whiting, would pass through Pepperell to Groton carrying dispatches from the British in Canada to the British in Boston. Since their men were out of town fighting in the war Sarah and a number of women in town armed themselves with muskets, pitchforks, and other weapons to guard the road into town. The women elected Prudence Wright as their leader.

The women put on men's clothing and gathered at Jewett's Bridge to await the rider. When he showed, they captured him and placed him under arrest and detained him at the house of Solomon Rodgers. The next day they turned their prisoner and the dispatches over to the Committee of Safety. See Prudence Cummings Wright in this book for more information.

Sources: 1. *Memorials of the Descendants of William Shattuck* by Lemuel Shattuck, 1855, pages 330-331. 2. D.A.R. Lineage Book, Vol. 7, page 326. 3. *History in the Making*, California State University, San Bernardino Journal of History, Vol. 9. 4. *An Encyclopedia of American Women at War: from the Home Front to the Battlefield*, pages 668-669. 5. D.A.R. Lineage Book, Vol. 29, page 187-188.

****

Mary Slocumb

Mary was born on February 11, 1760 in Bertie County, North Carolina, and she died on March 6, 1836 in Wayne County, North Carolina.

In February of 1776 Mary, just a young girl, was left alone when her husband Ezekiel Slocumb rode off to fight the local Tories in what would be called the Battle of Moore's Creek Bridge. Mary later recalled the day he left, *"I slept soundly and quietly that night and worked hard the next day; but I kept thinking where they had got to, how far, where and how many of the regulars and Tories they would meet; and I could not keep from that study."*

That night she went to sleep and had a terrible dream. She saw in the dream a body lying on the ground wrapped in her husband's cloak. She woke from the sleep, and her heart was beating wildly. *"If ever I felt fear it was at that moment,"* she remembered. Believing she must go to him, she left her baby with a friend, saddled her horse, and rode full speed down the road. By sunrise she had ridden thirty miles, when she encountered some people on the road. They were able to tell her in which direction the American troops had gone.

Around eight or nine in the morning she heard the fire of cannons, and she knew she was close to the battle. Soon she could hear muskets and then heard shouting. She was a few hundred yards from Moore's Bridge, and a few yards from the road in a cluster of trees she saw about twenty wounded men lying on the ground.

"I saw wrapped in his bloody guard cloak, my husband's body. I remember uncovering his head and seeing a face clothed with gore from a dreadful wound across the temple. I put my hand on the bloody face; 'twas warm; and an unknown voice gagged for water. A small camp kettle was lying near, and a stream of water close by. I brought it; poured some in his mouth; washed his face; and behold—it was Frank Cogdell."

Mary was washing his head wound, and Frank told her that it was the hole in his leg that was killing him. She stopped the bleeding and then went to the other men to dress their wounds. She became so busy with the wounded that she forgot to inquire about her husband. One of the officers came to her and she asked, *"Where is my husband?"*

She was told that Ezekiel was in pursuit of the enemy. The officer wanted to know why she was there. Mary replied, *"Oh, I thought you would need nurses as well as soldiers."* As she finished her husband came by. *"I would not tell my husband what brought me there. I was so happy; and so were all! It was a glorious victory; I came just at the height of the enjoyment. I knew my husband was surprised, but I could see he was not displeased with me."*

Mary preformed quite a feat that day. She aided the wounded men, probably saving several lives, and her ride to the battle was unbelievable. Mary had ridden alone, through the night, and through the wild country a distance of over 60 miles.

In April of 1781 British General Cornwallis encamped for several days on the river Neuse in North Carolina. The hated Colonel Banastre Tarleton took possession of the Slocumb plantation about 10 in the morning on a beautiful spring day. Mary, her daughter, her sister, and several slaves were the only people on the plantation at the time. Mary's husband, Lieutenant Ezekiel Slocumb was in the vicinity with his men scouting the camp of Cornwallis.

When Tarleton rode in he asked Mary if her husband was home. She replied, *"No sir he is in the army of his country, and fighting against our invaders."* Tarleton responded, *"Madam, the service of His Majesty requires the temporary occupation of your property; and if it would not be too great an inconvenience, I will take quarters in your house."*

Realizing she had no choice, Mary said, *"My family consist of only myself, my sister and child, and a few negroes. We are your prisoners."*

Mary prepared dinner for her uninvited guests, and during the meal conversation turned to the plantation. One of the British Captains remarked, *"When we conquer this country, is it not to be divided out among us?"* Tarleton answered the man, *"The officers of the army will undoubtedly receive large possessions of the conquered American provinces."*

75

Mary defiantly responded, *"Allow me to observe and prophesy. The only land in these United States which will ever remain in possession of a British officer, will measure but six feet by two."*

The conversation was interrupted by gunfire outside. Mary was fearful that her husband had returned home and was captured. She was relieved when she heard Tarleton order a patrol to be sent out to see about the gunfire. Mary sent a slave, Big George, out to where she thought her husband might be, in order to warn him on the presence of the British soldiers at the plantation.

Lieutenant Slocumb was leading a group of his men in pursuit of a band of Tories. As they neared the plantation they were intercepted by Big George. The slave stopped Slocumb in time, and the Americans were able to escape. Tarleton told Mary, *"Your husband made us a short visit, madam. I should have been happy to make his acquaintance, and that of his friend, Mr. Williams.* Mary was quick to reply, *"I have little doubt that you will meet the gentlemen, and they will thank you for the polite manner in which you treat their friends."*

When Mary was seventy-two she developed a cancer on her hand, and was told by the surgeon it must be removed with a knife. When it was time for the operation she refused to be held by the doctor's assistants. She told them, *"It is his business to cut out the cancer; I will take care of my arm."* She braced her arm on the table and never moved a muscle or made a sound during the operation. Mary died at the age of seventy-six.

Sources: 1. *History of North Carolina* by John H. Wheeler, Vol. 1, 1851, pages 457-460. 2. *Revolutionary Reader, Reminiscences and Indian Legends* complied by Sophie Lee Foster, D.A.R., 1913, pages 277-283. 3. *The Women of the American Revolution* by Elizabeth F. Ellet, Vol 1, 1819, pages 304-330. 4. *A History of the U.S. Army Nurse Corps* by Mary T. Sarnecky, 1999, page 7.

****

Elizabeth (Molly) Page Stark

Elizabeth was born on February 16, 1737 in Haverhill, Massachusetts, and she died on June 29, 1814 in New Hampshire. As a young girl she knew how to handle a gun, because she was often used as a guard at the fort to watch for Indians while her father and brothers were at work in the fields.

She married Major General John Stark on August 20, 1758. Her husband gained notoriety because of his battle call at the Battle of Bennington, *"There are your enemies, the Red Coats and the Tories. They are ours, or this night Molly Stark sleeps a widow!"*

When the news of the Battle of Concord and Lexington reached their house, her husband John left at once for the action. He left several necessary things behind, so Elizabeth gathered them up and rode after him. After riding many miles she joined him, gave him the items, and the next morning rode back home alone.

On one occasion she was alone at home with the children, when she heard the dogs barking outside the front door. She grabbed a rifle near the door and went outside to find a large bear in the front yard. She shot the bear, and the family had an ample supply of meat for the next few weeks.

Early in the war Elizabeth open her house to soldiers ill with smallpox during the winter while her husband and his men were encamped near Ticonderoga. She nursed the twenty men, including her own children back to health without losing a single patient.

During the evacuation of Boston by the British, General Washington ordered General Stark to capture the battery on Copp's Hill. The General ordered Elizabeth to ride into the countryside and arouse the people to join in the fight.

Elizabeth was described as a woman of strong and energetic character; eminently loving and kind to all, rich and poor alike; she shared her portion with any more needy than herself. Her obituary stated, *"Mrs. Stark retained her strength of mind and bodily health with scarce a day's sickness, from her youth, until attacked with a typhus fever on the 24th June, which terminated fatally on the 29th."*

Sources: 1. Obituary, 26 July, 1814 Portsmouth Gazette. 2. Vital Records of Haverhill, Massachusetts before 1749. 3. The American Monthly Magazine, Vol. 35, July-December, 1909, page 377-379. 4. D.A.R. American Revolution Magazine, Vol. 17, July-December, 1900, pages 348-350.

****

Elizabeth Steele

Elizabeth was born on October, 23, 1721 in Richmond County, Virginia, and she died on July 3, 1798 in Aiken County, South Carolina. Her first husband was Robert Gillespie who built a tavern to support his family. In 1763 Robert was murdered and scalped by Indians. Elizabeth then married William Steele, and the couple and their children continued to run the tavern. William died at thirty-nine years of age on November 1, 1773.

After the Battle of Cowpens, South Carolina on January 17, 1781, American General Nathanael Greene was attempting to gather his scattered army and procure equipment in order to attack and defeat British General Cornwallis. Greene arrived late at night at the tavern owned by Elizabeth. She heard the General say that he was tired, hungry, alone and penniless. He was also depressed, because he had recently learned of the death of his friend General William Davidson at the hands of the British.

Elizabeth served the General a warm meal and then presented him with two bags of either gold or silver. This was probably money that she had earned and saved over several years of hard work. This gift lifted the spirits of General Greene. Many years later the biographer of General Greene said, *"Never, did relief come at a more propitious moment; nor would it be straining conjecture to suppose that he resumed his journey with his spirits cheered and lightened by this touching proof of woman's devotion to the cause of her country."*

General Greene went on to gain control of South Carolina and eventually led Cornwallis toward Yorktown, where the British surrendered on October 19, 1781.

Sources: 1. *Daughters of America on Women of the Century*, by Phebe A. Hannaford, page 58. 2. *Women of the Revolution Vol. 1* by Elizabeth Ellet, pages 297-300.

****

Sally St. Clair

Sally was a young dark-eyed creole girl at the time of the Revolutionary War. Sometime just before or near the beginning of the war William Jasper had saved her life. Jasper joined the 2nd South Carolina Regiment as a sergeant and marched off to war. Sally's gratitude to William for saving her life turned to love, which she kept secret from him. William had a lover in

Pennsylvania, and after he became a sergeant he could afford to bring her to South Carolina and to marry.

Sally cut her hair and disguised her appearance, so that she could pass for a young boy and followed William into the army. William was unaware that the young soldier was Sally. She stayed as near William as she could during her time in the army, and no one suspected her of being a woman. Many times at night she would gaze upon William as he slept.

Sally and her secret love William both fought at the Siege of Savannah in the fall of 1779. She and William both died on October 9, 1779 during the battle. Sally's secret was discovered when her body was prepared for burial. George Pope Morris wrote a poem about Sally that begins:

In the ranks of Marion's band,
Through morass and wooded land,
Over beach of yellow sand,
Mountain, plain and valley;
A southern maid, in all her pride,
March'd gayly at her lover's side,
In such disguise
That e'en his eyes
Did not discover Sally.

IN THE MIDST OF THE BATTLE, WITH HER LOVER
BY HER SIDE, THE HEROIC MAIDEN DIES.

Illustration of Sally St. Clair from *Thrilling Adventures Among the Early Settlers* by W. Wildwood, 1866.

Sources: 1. *The Revolutionary War* by Charles Patrick Neimeyer, page 88. 2. *The Romance of the Revolution: being a History of the Personal Adventures, Romantic Incidents, and Exploits Incidental to the War of Independence*, pages 323-325. 3. *The Deserted Bride: and Other Poems* by George Pope Morris, pages 87-88. 4. *Thrilling Adventures among the Early Settlers* by Warren Wildwood, pages 78-81.

****

Anna Strong

Anna Strong, called Nancy by her friends, was born on April 14, 1740, and she died on August 12, 1812 in Setauket, New York. In November of 1760 she married Selah Strong, and they had eight children. Selah was an outspoken supporter of the patriot cause, and in 1778 he was arrested and sent to the prison ship *New Jersey*. The conditions on the prison ships were terrible and caused thousands of American deaths. Anna had some Tory relatives and was given permission to bring Selah food, which evidently saved his life. Her Tory relatives later helped her bribe British officials to release her husband.

Once freed Selah was paroled to live in Connecticut where he remained for the duration of the war. Anna stayed and worked the family farm in Seaton's Neck in Setauket. If she vacated the home, it would fall into disarray or be vandalized. Also, according to British law vacated homes could be confiscated by the British. The children probably stayed with Anna. One reason being there was less chance that she would be arrested, because then her children would be parentless. The older children ages seventeen, twelve, nine, and seven probably helped with the farm work, and taking care of the two younger boys ages three and less than one.

Soon the British troops took over her house and they forced Anna and her children to live alone in a tiny servant's house at the edge of their property on the shore of Little Bay. Her cabin was visible from Abraham Woodhull's house across Little Bay, which would later be beneficial.

The famous Culper Spy Ring began in September of 1778. Its purpose was to carry information of British operations in New York City to Setauket, across Long Island Sound to Fairfield, Connecticut, and then to General Washington. Major Benjamin Tallmadge, a Yale classmate of spy Nathan Hale, was placed in charge of the Culper Spy Ring. Tallmadge was ordered to recruit people into the ring who could be trusted.

The main people recruited included Caleb Brewster, an American Army officer, who had already been spying on the British, and Abraham Woodhull a childhood friend of both Brewster and Tallmadge. Woodhull would be the contact for Brewster. Robert Townsend, a friend of Abraham, would gather intelligence in New York City. Abraham and Robert had both lodged at a boarding house run by Abraham's brother-in-law. Last was Anna Strong, a friend of Abraham Woodhull and cousin of Caleb Brewster. She was selected to pass along messages by posting pre-arranged signals.

Each spy member was given a code name that even George Washington was not privileged to know. Abraham was given "Samuel Culper" or "Culper Sr." a variation of Culpeper County, Virginia, where Washington had worked as a young surveyor. Robert Townsend was "Samuel Culper, Jr." Tallmadge was referred to as "John Bolton." Brewster was agent 725 and the only member of the ring that the British later identified as a spy. George Washington was number 711. A possible lady member of the ring was identified as 355.

According to tradition, Anna would use her clothesline as a way to signal to Brewster and Abraham. If she hung a black petticoat, it meant that Brewster had arrived in town. Next to the petticoats would be a number of handkerchiefs. The specific number, one to six, would indicate one of the six hiding places where Brewster might be located. Abraham then would meet Brewster there or drop a message for him there.

A page from the code book of the Culper Spy Ring during the American Revolutionary War. On the left of the page are the names of people and places side-by-side with numbers that serve as their code representations.

Various mysteries surrounded Anna. The clothesline signal has never been verified, however, it was known that a woman in Setauket was under suspicion for disloyalty, and she fits Anna's description. On February 4, 1781 a double agent told the British that dispatches were sent from New York City by traitors in Setauket, where a man named Brewster received them *"near a certain woman."*

Also, was the lady member known as 355 Anna Strong or not? Was there even an agent 355? Some historians suggest that agent 355 was Sally Townsend the sister of Robert Townsend. Or perhaps Mary Underhill the sister of Abraham Woodhull.

In his book Washington's Spies: The Story of America's First Spy Ring, author Alexander Rose identifies agent 355 as Anna Strong, and that she died in 1812. This death date, however, is not consistent with the death date of other information about agent 355.

In the book George Washington's Secret Six: The Spy Ring That Saved the American Revolution by Brian Kilmeade and Don Yaeger, they wrote that agent 355 was a younger woman who was acquainted with Major John Andre. Mary Underhill, Abraham's sister, was in her thirties and did supply information about the activities of Major John Andre.

A third book, Gallantry in Action: A Biographic Dictionary of Espionage in the American Revolutionary War by Henry Thayer Mahoney and Marjorie Locke Mahoney, reports that agent 355 had access to British headquarters but identified her as the mistress and common law wife of Robert Townsend "Samuel Culper Jr." They also stated that she died in 1780 during childbirth while confined on a British prison ship.

The mistress as agent 355 first appeared in 1948 in a book by Morton Pennypacker, a Suffolk County historian. He wrote of a female spy that had Townsend's child and later died on a prison ship. He had little evidence to back up his story.

Estelle D. Lockwood in the Long Island Forum, The Lady Known as 355 dismissed the mistress story. She wrote that the lifelong bachelor, Robert Townsend, did have a son born out of wedlock. The mother was Mary Banvard, a housekeeper for Robert. Also, Robert Jr. was not born until February 1, 1784, which was after the war had ended and long after the spy ring was dissolved. Some historians have also suggested that Robert Sr. was raising his brother's child.

So, where did the idea begin that there was an agent 355 in the first place? The only hint that there was a woman agent 355 came from a single line in a coded letter to Washington dated August 15, 1779 from "Culper Sr." *I intended to visit 727* (code for New York) *before long and think by the assistance of a 355* (code for lady) *of my acquaintance, shall be able to outwit them all.*" The letter mentions "a 355," not an agent 355. The word lady in their code was 355, just like 371 was a man, and 195 was a father. It was possible that the lady in question could have been Anna Strong because at the time her husband was on a prison ship in New York City and she was allowed to visit him. If Anna was present with Abraham it would divert attention from him. They would appear to be just another couple traveling to visit friends or relatives.

Whatever role Anna Strong played in the ring, she did risk her life for the cause. Her husband appeared on the list of people to be reimbursed while he was in prison. Perhaps it was actually reimbursement to Anna for her expenses while serving in the spy ring. After the war the people in the spy ring remained anonymous.

On April 22, 1790 President Washington stayed at the Roe Tavern in Setauket and met with Selah Strong. When he left the next morning he said, *"The Roe Tavern was tolerably decent with obliging people in it."* While there it was never reported if he met with any of the former members of the Culper Spy Ring.

It wasn't until 1939 that Morton Pennypacker discovered the true identity of "Culper Jr." as being Robert Townsend. He had a handwriting expert compare family papers written by Townsend to those of Culper Jr.'s spy letters. The handwriting of the two groups of papers matched.

Sources: 1. *The Lady Known as "355"* by Estelle D. Lockwood, pages 10-15. 2. *Gallantry in Action: A Biographic Dictionary of Espionage in the American Revolutionary War* by Henry Thayer Mahoney and Marjorie Locke Mahoney, page 304. 3. *Washington's Spies: The Story of America's First Spy Ring* by Alexander Rose, page 75. 4. *George Washington's Secret Six: The Spy Ring That Saved the American Revolution* by Brian Kilmeade and Don Yaeger, page 58. 5. *In Disguise!: Undercover with Real Women Spies* by Ryan Ann Hunter. 6. *Sally Townsend, George Washington's Teenage Spy* by Paul R. Misencik, pages 100-101. 7. *An Encyclopedia of American Women at War: From the Home Front to the Battlefields, Vol. 1* by Lisa Tendrich Frank. 8. *The Diary of George Washington from 1789 to 1791*, edited by Benson J. Lossing, page 124.

****

Sarah Tarrant

British Lieutenant Colonel William Leslie led an attack on Salem, Massachusetts on February 26, 1776, which was nearly two months before the Battle of Concord and Lexington. The purpose of the attack was to seize provisions, gunpowder, and cannons that the patriots had stored there. As the British marched on Salem that cold Sunday morning, the alarm quickly went out through the town. The 240 British regulars, with the drum and fife corps playing Yankee Doodle, marched toward the bridge over the North River at Salem.

Colonel Mason of the American militia had the northern leaf of the drawbridge raised to stop the British. On the south side of the bridge stood the American minutemen armed with muskets, pitchforks, and clubs defiantly facing the British regulars.

Colonel Leslie called out to the Americans, *"I am determined to pass over this bridge before I return to Boston, if I remain here until next autumn."*

Captain Felt of the American militia replied, *"Nobody would care for that."*

The British Colonel yelled back, *"By God, I will not be defeated."* Captain Felt answered, *"You must acknowledge that you have been already baffled."*

Colonel Leslie then said that he was on the King's highway, and he would not be prevented from passing freely over it. An old man in the crowd yelled back to the Colonel, *"It is not the King's highway, it was built by the owners of the lots on the other side, and no king, county, or town has any control over it."*

As the day was drawing to a close, Colonel Leslie proposed that he be allowed to cross the bridge and pass a few yards beyond it, and then he would turn around and cross back over it and leave. His orders were to cross the bridge, and he did not want to disobey orders. Both sides agreed to the conditions, and the drawbridge was lowered and the British quietly passed over it. Many of the town's people, however, were still angered by the appearance of the British in their town.

Looking out the window of a house near the bridge was a nurse named Sarah Tarrant. She yelled out to the British troops, *"Go home and tell your master he has sent you on a fool's errand, and has broken the peace of our Sabbath; what do you think we were born in the woods, to be frighten by owls?"* This was a common expression of the time and was meant to indicate that the speaker was use to danger and could not be easily frightened.

This angered one of the British soldiers, so he raised his musket and aimed it at Sarah. Showing no fear she hollered at the soldier, *"Fire if you have the courage, but I doubt it."*

No one chose to do any firing that day, and Colonel Leslie and his men retreated back to their ship. Later, the Colonel was court martialed for his failure to perform his mission. If the British soldier had opened fire that day it could have resulted in firing on both sides. That would have resulted in the Revolutionary War starting in Salem and not in Concord and Lexington almost two months later.

Sources: 1. A *Glossary of Words & Phrases Usually Relating to the U.S.* by John Russell Bartlett, 1860. 2. *Account of Leslie's Retreat at the North Bridge in Salem* by Charles M. Endicott, 1856, pages 17-31.

****

Jane Black Thomas

Jane was born in 1720 in Chester County, Pennsylvania, and she died on April 11, 1811 in Greenville County, South Carolina. Jane was described as a woman of considerable beauty, with black eyes and hair, and a fair complexion. The following obituary appeared in the *Carolina Gazette* in Charleston, South Carolina on May 25, 1811,

> *"DIED, on the 16th of April, in the 91st year of her age, Mrs. Jane Thomas, wife of Col. John Thomas. She was descended from respectable parents of the name of Black, in the state of Pennsylvania, was an useful member of society, and a pious christian of the Presbyterian persuasion, The husband of her youth is left, dove like, to lament his irreparable loss, and though old and decriped, he feels it most sensibly--Her children, grand-children and great- grand children, are very numerous; while they lament their loss, they are consoled with the hope that she is gone to the friend of sinners Jesus Christ. She was a sincere and spirited whig. In the year 1779, when the tories attacked the house of her husband, to get at a magazine kept there, she cooperated with her son and son-in-law in guarding it. While they fired on the assailants, she advanced in front of them, with a sword in her hand and dared them to come on. They were intimidated and retired. She steadily refused to drink any tea after the revolutionary war commenced, saying "it was the blood of some of the poor men who first fell in the war." She enjoyed good health throughout her long life, lived on a spare diet, with frequent draughts of butter-milk, but never took any physic."*

Jane's husband John was the commander of the area's loyalist militia in the 1750's. When the Revolution began, he resigned his English commission and formed the Patriot's Spartan Regiment. The patriots had stored ammunition at the Thomas two story home since 1776, and in 1780 the Tories decided to confiscate it.

Colonel Thomas was with his men fighting in Charlestown, and to guard the ammunition he left twenty-five men under the command of his son, Captain John Thomas Jr. Staying at the house was Jane, three of her daughters, and her youngest son. The Tories under Colonel Patrick Moore, and 150 or more men advanced toward the house. Captain Thomas and his men gathered as much of the ammunition and they could and left to hide it. The people Captain Thomas left behind in the house to guard the remaining ammunition were Jane, her children, and son-in-law Josiah Culbertson.

As the Tories arrived, they were met with musket fire from the house. Inside Jane and her children formed a production line and were loading muskets, and they gave them to Culbertson so quickly that the Tories thought there were several men inside firing at them. Jane was seen in the doorway with a sword in her hand and daring the Tories to come in. The Tories finally retreated, and the much needed ammunition was saved.

Later in June of 1780 Jane's husband and two of her sons were imprisoned by the Tories in a brick jail. She went to visit them, and while there overheard a conversation between two Tory women. *"Tomorrow night the Loyalist intent to surprise the Rebels at Cedar Spring."*

Cedar Spring was only a few miles from Jane's house, so she mounted her horse and rode off to warn the patriots. When she reached the American camp, the rebels made preparations to set a trap for the Tories. That night 150 Tories attacked the American camp and the sixty Americans were waiting for them. Thanks to Jane's warning the Americans won a victory even though outnumbered two to one.

Sources: 1. *The Women of the American Revolution* by Elizabeth F. Ellet, Vol. 1, 1819, pages 250-260. 2. *The Part Taken by Women in American History* by Mrs. John A. Logan, 1912, pages 181-183. 3. *History of Spartanburg County, South Carolina* by Dr. John B.O. Landrum, 1900, page 188.

****

Sarah Townsend

Sarah Townsend lived in Oyster Bay, Long Island. Her brother Robert was a spy for General George Washington, and he was working under the pseudonym of "Culper Junior" in the famous Culper spy ring. During the Revolutionary War her house was occupied by Colonel John Simcoe of the British army.

One day Sarah saw a strange man in her kitchen, and he placed a letter in the cupboard, and then left the house. She got the letter and saw it was addressed to John Anderson, and she looked at the contents which meant nothing to her. She did not know that John Anderson was the pseudonym for British Major John Andre. She later saw Andre go to the cupboard and take the letter.

That evening she overheard a conversation between Andre and Simcoe, and she heard the words "West Point." Since West Point was an important American fort, she sent a message to her brother Robert. Sarah did not know that General Benedict Arnold was planning on turning West Point over to the British.

Robert informed General Washington of what Sarah had seen and heard. Later Andre was captured, and the plans to capture West Point were exposed. In a small way Sarah had saved West Point.

Sources: 1. *Gallantry in Action: A Biographic Dictionary of Espionage in the American Revolutionary War* by Harry Mahoney and Marjorie Locke Mahoney. 2. *Women Patriots of the American Revolution: a Biographical Dictionary* by Charles E. Claghorn.

****

Unknown Woman

The following story was told by two Revolutionary officers to the Rev. J. H. Saye. It occurred in the early part of the Revolutionary War on the frontier of Burke County, North Carolina. The inhabitants of the area feared an Indian attack and were going to seek protection in the fort several miles away. A group of soldiers were sent to protect the settlers, as they made their way to the fort.

The settlers had traveled several miles, with the soldiers marching in a square with the settlers in the center. Their road led to a dense forest, where the Indians were hidden and waiting for them. As the settlers approached, the Indians fired on them and a battle began.

During the fight a cry rang out from the soldiers, *"Our powder is giving out. Bring us some or we can fight no longer."* One of the women in the group of settlers spread her apron on the ground, and others began to pour powder into it. She then went from soldier to soldier and poured powder in their hats, while in full view of the Indians and putting her life at risk. She went to each soldier until her supply of powder was exhausted. Soon the soldiers were able to drive the Indians off and save the settlers.

The soldiers began to ask where the woman was that gave them the powder. Several of the men exclaimed, *"Where is she, we want to see her. Without her we should have all been lost."* Since they did not see her they feared that she had been killed. One of the men then said, *"You are looking in the wrong place."* He pointed toward a large tree many yards away. At the base of the tree was the woman on her knees in prayer. Rather than accepting the thanks of her friends, she was giving thanks to Heaven for their deliverance.

Source: 1. *Women of the Revolution Vol. 1.* by Elizabeth Ellet, pages 162-163.

****

Martha Lott Van Doren

Martha was born in 1728 in Middlebush, New Jersey, and she died there on October 21, 1815. George Washington spent many nights at the home of Martha and John Van Doren in New Jersey. Knowing this, the British visited their home one day and took Martha prisoner and demanded information about the patriot army. Martha refused, to give any information, so the British hung her by her heels to force her to talk. She still refused and when her faced started to turn black they released her. The British left without getting any information.

Sources: 1. Sons of the American Revolution Application. 2. D.A.R. Lineage Book, Vol. 146, page 281.

****

Catherine Van Winkle

Catherine Van Winkle was born on June 1, 1763 in Hudson County, New Jersey, and she died there on December 5, 1863. The following occurred on September 15, 1776 and is from her obituary in the *American Standard*, Jersey City December 16, 1863:

"From the steeple of the old church at south Bergen, she beheld the British fleet take possession of the city of New York, and not long after, she saw King George's army march past her father's house on its way to Philadelphia. About this time the British took possession of her father's house—converting it into an arsenal, and they made an attempt to hang her father, because he would not disclose the whereabouts of money which he was supposed to be possessed of. After swinging him from a beam in the house, they left him for dead; but, fortunately, the last spark had not fled, and his life was saved by being cut down by the daughter who is the subject of this notice. While the British were operating in

this vicinity, she performed one of those heroic acts for which the women of those trying times were celebrated, in carrying a message, under perilous circumstances, to a section of the American army encamped at Belleville, informing the commandant of a designed night attack upon his forces by the British, and thus giving him time to frustrate the designs."

Catherine and her younger sister Maria often carried messages from Lafayette to General Washington at Belleville, which was a distance of about seven miles. On one occasion they walked there in the night to warn Washington of a British plot to surround and capture him.

The quick wit of the two girls saved the life of an American soldier one time. The soldier was at their father's house, when a party of British soldiers surrounded their house in search of him. The girls quickly hid him between the feather and straw beds of their own beds, and then they went to bed. When the British soldiers entered their room to search for the soldier, the girls pretended to be asleep. The soldiers poked under the bed with their bayonets and searched other areas of the room. Convinced that the American soldier was not in the house they left.

Appreciative of the loyalty of the family, over the years Washington would visit Catherine's father's house for dinner. On August 26, 1782 Catherine married George Shepherd, who had served in the New Jersey Militia.

Sources: 1. *Jersey City and Its Historical Sites* by Harriet Phillips Eaton by James Langston 2. *Women Patriots of the American Revolution: a Biographical Dictionary* by Charles E. Claghorn.

****

Nanyehi aka Nancy Ward

Nancy was born c. 1738 in Chota, near present-day Knoxville, Tennessee, and she died c. 1822. She was a Beloved Woman of the Cherokee Indians, which meant she was allowed to sit in councils and make decisions with the Chiefs and other Beloved Women.

She was with her husband Tsu-la, when he was killed in a battle against the Creeks in 1755. Nancy laid behind a log, in order to chew his bullets so that the resulting jagged edges might do more damage to the victim. When Tsu-la was killed, she picked up his rifle and fought in his place during the Cherokee victory. Because of her bravery she was appointed Ghighau, the head Beloved Woman. She later mediated peace relations with the white settlers in the area, and also with the British and American governments during the Revolutionary War.

One time she warned the white people of the Watauga area about an impending attack against them by another Cherokee tribe. When Mrs. Lydia Bean was taken captive by the Cherokees she refused to tell of the

Painted in 1836 by George Catlin

conditions inside the settler's fort, so she was tied to a stake and condemned to be burned alive. Nancy intervened to save Mrs. Bean's life. She arrived in camp just as the fire was lit. In gratitude Mrs. Bean taught Nancy how to make butter and a new loom weaving technique. Besides being a negotiator of peace, Nancy also introduced the tribe to farming and dairy production which brought great changes to the Cherokee society.

Later, Nancy married Bryant Ward and had a daughter Betsy, who later married General Joseph Martin. Bryant was already married to a white woman and ended up returning to live with her. He still maintained close relations with Nancy over the years.

In the summer of 1781 Nancy negotiated a peace treaty between the Cherokees and the Americans. During the negotiations Nancy said, *"You know that women are always looked upon as nothing; but we are your mothers; you are our sons. Our cry is all for peace; let it continue. This peace must last forever. Let your women's sons be ours. Let our sons be yours. Let your women hear our words."* This treaty allowed the Americans to send more troops to Washington's army against the British General Cornwallis.

Sources: 1. *Native Women's History in Eastern North America Before 1900* edited by Rebecca Kugel, Lucy Eldersveld Murphy, pages, 99-100. 2. *Women in Early America: Struggle, Survival, and Freedom in a New World* by Dorothy A. Mays, pages 411-412, 2004. 3. *The Cherokee People: The Story of the Cherokees from Earliest Origins to Contemporary Times* by Thomas E. Mails, pages 193-194, 1992. 4. *The Columbia Guide to American Indians of the Southeast* by Theda Michael Green, page 216, 2001.

****

Hannah Watts Weston

Hannah Watts was born on November 22, 1758 in Haverhill, Massachusetts, and she died on December 12, 1854 in Washington County, Maine. Hannah moved with her family to Maine, and in October of 1774 she married Josiah Weston. Hannah and Josiah settled in Jonesboro about sixteen miles from Machias, Maine.

News of the battle at Lexington and Concord reached Machias later in April. Josiah was a member of the Council of War, which met one day in May at Burnham Tavern to discuss the events and what action should be taken. They voted to plant a "Tree of Liberty", which would be a symbol of their belief in self-government and freedom from tyranny. These symbols had been planted in other colonies for the past few years. Once planted the people would gather around and pledge their support against England.

In June of 1775 news reached the people of Jonesboro that a British ship was coming the next day to capture the town of Machias. About twenty men assembled at the home of Josiah. Included with the men were the father and two brothers of Hannah. While the men were waiting at the house Hannah talked with them about ammunition, means of defense, and what they would leave behind.

After the men left Hannah called around to several families, and she gathered all the powder, lead, pewter spoons, and such that could be found. *"We must melt these and make bullets for the men of Machias,"* shouted Hannah. *"If there be not time to melt them, these pewter dishes must go as they are."*

By early next morning, she had accumulated about thirty to forty pounds of supplies that needed to be taken to Machias. She learned that one of the men had returned, and she thought he would be the likely choice to transport the supplies. When she went to his house she learned that he had taken flight to the woods to hide from the British.

Hannah's sister-in-law Rebecca offered to help her take to Machias the pillow case full of materials to make ammunition. Early in the morning the two of them went sixteen miles to Machias. Hannah was seventeen, five months pregnant, and carried the supplies. Rebecca was fifteen, and carried a hatchet, and their food. After the first five miles they became lost and stopped to rest and eat.

They again began their travel after a short rest period, and about two in the afternoon they came upon the river that would lead them to Machias. By following the river they hoped to reach the town before dark. They had to move through some thick swamps, and Rebecca grew tired. So in addition to the ammunition, Hannah also carried the food.

After two or three hours they were at the foot of a high hill, and not knowing for sure where they were. They rested for about an hour as the sun began to set. Hannah told Rebecca to remain with the supplies while she climbed the hill to see where they were. With the aid of a walking stick Hannah was able to ascend to the top of the hill. She discovered that one of the houses of Manchias was not that far off.

Hannah hurried back down the hill to get Rebecca and the supplies. The two girls climbed the hill and hurried toward the house before it grew too dark to travel. They reached the house of Gideon O'Brien just in time, because Rebecca was very tired and had become ill. Hannah was completely exhausted and was thankful that she would be able to rest inside the house. Surrounding neighbors came to the house where the two girls were staying, and they helped take care of them and to melt the supplies they brought into musket balls.

The next morning the girls learned what had happen in Manchias the proceeding day. The British ship, *Margaretta,* landed her troops. The British officer in charge ordered the town to remove their "Liberty Tree" from the town square, or in the words of the ship's captain, *"We will fire on the town."*

So many men had come to the aid of the town, that the British were outnumbered. Therefore, the Americans captured the ship, thus saving the town. The townspeople were very appreciative of the bravery and perseverance of the two girls. The girls also received the thanks of the leaders of the militia and they were given a gift of twelve yards of "Camlet", a cloth which the girls later made into dresses.

Hannah was disappointed that the ammunition she and Rebecca brought would not be used and she felt their work was for nothing. Captain O'Brien of the militia replied, *"This pewter is in the nick of time, for I warn you before many days be passed the English will be upon us again. And, Mistress Weston, I promise your bullets shall do good work when our visitors come."* The next day the two girls and the men of Jonesboro returned home by water. The bullets were later used in repulsing attacks on the town of Machias.

Sources: 1. *The Revolution, Life of Hannah Weston* by George W. Drisko, pages 5, 55-62. 2. *The Part Taken by Women in America History* by Mrs. John A. Logan, pages 158-160. 3. *Narrative of the Town of Machias* by George W. Drisko, pages 34-45.

****

Mrs. Whitall

At the Battle of Red Bank on October 22, 1777 over 600 Americans repelled 900 Hessian troops who were trying to take Fort Mercer. During the battle, Mrs. Whitall was in a room in her home inside the fort. She was on the second floor spinning on her wheel and trying to pass the time during the battle. A British cannon ball entered the attic just above her. The cannon ball rolled across the floor, down the stairs, and landed at the foot of the stairs no more than 10 feet from where she was sitting. She got up, took her spinning wheel to the basement, and continued her spinning.

Sources: 1. *D.A.R. Lineage Book, Vol. 34.* 2. *Forty Minutes by the Delaware "The Battle of Fort Mercer"* by Lee Patrick Anderson.

****

Eleanor Carruthers Wilson

Eleanor Carruthers Wilson was born c. 1724 in Cumberland County, Pennsylvania, and she died before April 26, 1802 in Mecklenburg County, North Carolina. She married Robert Wilson, and they had eleven sons with seven serving in the American Revolution along with their father.

Two of the sons, Robert Jr. and Joseph, were taken prisoners at the surrender of Charleston and were later allowed to return home. Once at home, rather than being forced to join the Tory militia, they enlisted again in the American army. In one battle Joseph encountered a Tory militiaman that he knew in hand-to-hand combat. He killed the Tory after a severe struggle and carried off the dead man's rifle. Robert Sr. and his son John were later captured and placed in jail in Camden. One of their jail mates was Andrew Jackson, the future president.

In October of 1780 General Cornwallis and his troops stopped at the Wilson plantation and began stealing provisions. Cornwallis soon learned that this was the home of a patriot leader who had seven sons in the rebel army. Cornwallis encouraged Mrs. Wilson to have her husband and sons join the British army,

"Madam, your husband and your son are my prisoners; the fortune of war may soon place others of your sons-perhaps all your kinsmen, in my power. Your sons are young, aspiring and brave. In a good cause, fighting for a generous and powerful king, such as George III, they might hope for rank, honor and wealth. If you could but induce your husband and sons to leave the rebels, and take up arms for their lawful sovereign, I would almost pledge myself that they shall have rank and consideration in the British army. If you, madam, will pledge yourself to induce them to do so, I will immediately order their discharge."

Mrs. Wilson replied, *"I have seven sons who are now, or have been bearing arms. Indeed my seventh son, Zaccheus, who is only fifteen years old, I yesterday assisted to get ready to go and join his brothers in Sumter's army. Now sooner than see one of my family turn back from the glorious enterprise, I would take these boys* [pointing to three or small sons] *and with them would myself enlist under Sumter's standard, and show my husband and sons how to fight, and if necessary to die for their country."*

The cruel Lieutenant Colonel Banastre Tarleton turned to General Cornwallis and sneered, *"Ah! General! I think you've gotten into a hornet's nest! Never mind, when we get to Camden, I'll take good care that old Robert Wilson never comes back again!"* He apparently knew that Robert Wilson Sr. was in jail at Camden.

The next day the British army moved out, and a group of scouts captured Zaccheus who was found on the flank of the British with his rifle. It appeared that he was preparing to lie in wait and ambush some of the enemy. He was taken to Cornwallis, who demanded that the boy act as a guide. He wanted the young boy to show him the best place to cross the Catawba River. When the British reached the river, Zaccheus showed them the best place to cross. Some of the British troops were half way across, when they found themselves in deep water and were swept down river by the strong current.

Cornwallis, red with rage, drew his sword and said he was going to cut the boy's head off for his treachery. Zaccheus faced him and replied, *"I have no arms and I am your prisoner. You have the power to kill me."* He then added, *"But Sir, don't you think it would be a cowardly act for you to strike an unarmed boy with your sword. If I had but half of your weapon, it would not be so cowardly, but then you know you would not be so safe."*

Cornwallis was impressed with the lad's courage and said to him, *"You are a fine fellow, and I would not hurt a hair on your head. Go home and take care of your mother and tell her to keep her boys at home."* If this exchange had taken place between Zaccheus and Colonel Tarleton, the young boy would have likely been killed on the spot.

Later sometime in November Cornwallis, sent word to the prison to have Robert, his son John, and several other men released from jail in Camden. Once released they were to be safely transported to a prison in Charleston. Before the guards arrived to release them, Robert organized the men to escape. When the prisoners overpowered their guards, Robert Wilson made the guards swear never again to bear arms against the rebels and sent them on their way with a warning, *"If I ever find a single mother son of you in arms again, I will hang you up to a tree like a dog."* With people like the Wilsons, it is no wonder that the rebels won their freedom from Great Britain.

Eleanor and her husband lived to a ripe old age at Steele Creek. Robert died in 1794, and Eleanor died about 1802. It is estimated that their descendants, living in Tennessee and the West, now number seven or eight hundred.

Sources: 1. *Women of the Revolution, Vol. III, Chapter XX, 1852* by Elizabeth F. Ellett, pages 347-356. 2. *Women of the Frontier* by Billy Kennedy. 3. *Women of the Century* by Phebe Ann Hannaford.

****

Prudence Cummings Wright

In the spring of 1775 Prudence Cummings Wright was thirty five years old and the mother of seven children. She lived with her husband David in Pepperell, Massachusetts. The British government considered Massachusetts the most rebellious of the thirteen colonies. There was no standing army in Massachusetts at this time, but what they did have were citizen soldiers called Minutemen.

These Minutemen had a network of messengers and signals that could alert the towns of any danger approaching them. When the men went off to fight, their wives remained behind and molded bullets, gathered supplies, and tended to the chores at home. In some cases they also got involved as soldiers.

Early in the morning of April 19, 1775 news that the redcoats and patriots had fought at Lexington reached the home of David and Prudence Wright. They also learned that the British were now advancing toward Concord. The Colonel of the local militia alerted the men of Pepperell to meet him at Groton, which was a little over five miles away. The men grabbed their muskets, powder horns, a few supplies, and kissed their families good-bye not knowing if they would return.

While her husband was with the Minutemen, Prudence was visiting her mother in Hollis, New Hampshire almost six miles away. While there she overheard some local Tories, who were friendly to the British, discussing plans to send messages between the British in the north and the British in Boston. She realized that the road the Tories would take between the north and Boston passed through the town of Pepperell.

The men of Pepperell were harassing the British troops as they marched back to the safety of Boston, so Prudence realized that it would be up to the women to stop the Tories from sending messages. Prudence returned to Pepperell and called to arms the 30 to 40 women remaining in town. The women dressed in their men's clothing and gathered weapons, and they elected Prudence as the commander of their militia company. Prudence chose seventeen year old Sarah Hartwell Shattuck as her lieutenant, and the newly formed company stood ready for a fight armed with muskets, pitchforks, and any other tool that could be used as a weapon.

The women gathered at the bridge over the Nashua River, which was just outside of Pepperell on the road to Hollis. The women guarded the bridge, patrolled the road, and swore that no foe to freedom should pass that bridge. The company of women, who became known as the Prudence Wright Guard, hoped that if British troops showed up that they could scare the troops off, before it was discovered that the patriots facing them were women.

The bridge was located out in the country with no homes nearby. The road to the bridge curved around an area of high ground, so that the bridge could not be seen until you were nearly on it, if you were traveling from the north. The women waited all night in silence waiting for the enemy. Late in the night two riders approached the bridge, and Prudence jumped out in front of them and shone her lantern into their eyes. She demanded to know who they were and at what business they were on. When the startled men tried to escape, the company of women surrounded them and grabbed the reins of the horses.

One rider, Captain Leonard Whiting, was a well know Tory in the area and drew his pistol, and he was about to fire it. The other rider, also a Tory, was Samuel Cummings who was the brother of Prudence. Samuel told the Captain to lower his weapon, when he recognized his sister's voice. He told the Captain that his sister, *"would wade through blood for the rebel cause."* The two men dismounted, were searched, and dispatches from the British troops in the north to the British in Boston were found in Samuel's boot. The prisoners were taken to a local home and guarded the rest of the night.

In the morning the women took their prisoners to Groton and turned them over to the Committee of Safety. The documents found on them were sent on to Charlestown. The two prisoners were later released on the condition that they never return to Massachusetts. Some versions of this story indicate that it was the other brother of Prudence, Thomas, rather than Samuel who was captured. Both of her brothers were Tories, and they left the area never to be seen by the family again. On March 19, 1777 town officials voted to award the women at the bridge seven pounds, seventeen shillings, and six pence for their services during the war.

Sources: 1. *Memorials of the Descendants of William Shattuck* by Lemuel Shattuck, 1855, pages 330-331. 2. D.A.R. Lineage Book, Vol. 7, page 326. 3. *History in the Making, California State University, San Bernardino Journal of History, Vol. 9.* 4. *An Encyclopedia of American Women at War: from the Home Front to the Battlefield*, pages 668-669.

****

Mary "Polly" Wyckoff

Polly Wyckoff was born in February of 1770 in Allentown, New Jersey, and she was buried there. On the night of November 19, 1776 three Tories guided the British forces across the Hudson River and up the Palisades, in an attempt to attack the American soldiers at Fort Lee in New Jersey. Polly was visiting friends in Bogartsfield and spotted the British troops on the morning of November 20th. The troops had just climbed the Palisades and were marching southward toward Fort Lee.

Polly ran into the friend's house and told her mother what she had seen. Her mother passed the warning on to Peter Bogart, who rode to warn the American troops that the British were going to attack. The next day 2,000 American troops retreated across the Hackensack River and made their way to Hackensack. They took all the boats and destroyed bridges on their retreat. The Americans lost their supplies at Fort Lee, but the British failed to capture Washington and the American troops. It was during this retreat that Thomas Paine wrote *The American Crisis*, which began, *"These are the times that try men's souls."*

Sources: 1. *Historical Collections of the State of New Jersey* by John W. Barber and Henry Howe, 1844. 2. *Women Patriots of the American Revolution: a Biographical Dictionary* by Charles E. Claghorn.

****

Elizabeth Zane

Elizabeth Zane was born on July 19, 1765 in Berkeley County, Virginia, and she died on August 23, 1823. Her bravery is immortalized in a book written in 1903 by her descendant, Zane Grey, entitled *Betty Zane*.

Elizabeth and her family moved into the area that is now Wheeling, West Virginia. The family and several others established Fort Henry in this wilderness. It was surrounded by thick woods, and the Indians in the area were very much pro-British. On September 11, 1782 Fort Henry was attacked by British and their Indian allies.

The fort had only about sixteen fighting men, and the rest were women and children. During the attack, Elizabeth occupied the sentry box with her brother Jonathan and John Saltar. Her job was to load the guns for the two men. The people inside the fort were facing over 300 enemy fighters. The supply of powder soon dwindled to just a few loads left.

Elizabeth's brother Ebenezer remembered that he had carelessly left a keg of gunpowder back at their home, which was about sixty yards from the fort's gate. Colonel Zane, Elizabeth's father, called the men together and said that someone who was a fast runner would need to go for the powder. He reminded them of the danger of the journey and said there would be a good chance the runner would be shot down by the enemy.

Several of the boys volunteered. However, the Colonel was hesitant to let them leave. They could not afford to lose any of the fighting men, so Elizabeth knowing this volunteered. She told her father she was aware of the danger, but her loss would be less important than if a fighting man was to fall. She told her father, *"You have not one man to spare; a woman will not be missed in the defense of the fort."*

The men opened the gate, and Elizabeth stepped outside and began walking at a fast pace. The Indians looked at her and did not consider her any threat, and several of them yelled, *"Squaw, Squaw"* as she passed by. She quickly made it to the house, tied a tablecloth around her waist, and poured the powder in it. As she started back to Fort Henry, the enemy realized what this girl was up to and began firing. Ball after ball whizzed past her as she ran back to the fort. She entered the fort unharmed with only one musket ball hole in her dress. About two days later a relief force was sent, and the Indians and British retreated. Her feat is even more impressive, because she had gone without sleep for the past forty hours.

Lithograph by Nagel and Weingaertner from Library of Congress. "Heroism of Miss Elizabeth Zane."

Sources: 1. *Young and Brave: Girls Changing History.* 2. *The Women of the American Revolution, Vol. 2* by Elizabeth Fries Ellet. 3. Elizabeth Zane Chapter, West Virginia State Society, D.A. R. 4. *Some Pennsylvania Women during the War of the Revolution,* edited by William Henry Egle.

****

BIBLIOGRAPHY

_____, *American Genealogical Biographical Index Vol. 34*. Published under the auspices of an Advisory Committee representing the cooperating subscribing libraries by Godfrey Memorial Library.

The American Monthly Magazine, Vol. 35, July-December, 1909.

Anderson County Museum Advisory Committee selections for the hall of Fame Class in 2015.

Anderson, Laurie Halse, *Independent Dames: What You Never Knew About the Women and Girls of the Revolution*. New York, New York: Simon & Schuster, 2008.

Anderson, Lee Patrick, *Forty Minutes by the Delaware "The Battle of Fort Mercer"*. Irvine, California: Universal Publishers, 1999.

The Ann Simpson Davis Chapter, Daughters of the American Revolution.

_____, *Article in The Pittsburgh Press, Sunday August 2, 1953*.

Bakeless, John, *Turncoats, Traitors, and Heroes*. New York, New York: J.B. Lippincott & Co., 1959.

Barber, John W. and Henry Howe, *Historical Collections of the State of New Jersey*, New York, New York: S. Tuttle, 1844.

Bartlett, John Russell, *A Glossary of Words & Phrases Usually Relating to the U.S.* Boston, Massachusetts: Little Brown & Company, 1860.

Beirne, Francis F., *The Amiable Baltimoreans*. Baltimore, Maryland: The Johns Hopkins University Press, 1951.

Berkin, Carol, *Revolutionary Mothers: Women in the Struggle for America's Independence*. New York, New York: Alfred A. Knoff, 2005.

Betsy Dowdy Chapter of the D.A.R. Elizabeth City, North Carolina.

Bohrer, Melissa Lukeman, *Glory, Passion, and Principal: the Story of Eight Remarkable Women at the Core of the American Revolution*. New York, New York: Atria Books, 2003.

Boudinot, Elias, *Journal or Historical Recollections of American Events during the Revolutionary War*. Trenton, New Jersey: C.L. Traver, 1890.

Bracken, Jeanne Munn, *Women in the American Revolution*. Boston, Massachusetts: History Compass, 2009.

Brown, Meredith Mason, *Frontiersman: Daniel Boone and the Making of America*. Baton Rouge, Louisiana: Louisiana State University Press, 2008.

Buchanan, John, *The Road to Guilford Courthouse: The American Revolution in the Carolinas*. New York, New York: John Wiley & Sons, 1999.

Bunce, Oliver Bell, *The Romance of the Revolution: Being True Stories of Adventure, Romantic Incidents, Hairbreadth Escapes, and Heroic Exploits of the Days of '76*. Philadelphia, Pennsylvania: Porter and Coats, 1870.

Burgess, Louis Alexander, *Virginia Soldiers of 1776*. Richmond, Virginia: Clearfield Company, 1927.

Byerly, Thomas and Joseph Clinton Robertson, *The Percy Anecdotes Vol. 2, 1834*. New York, New York: Harper and Brothers, 1834.

The Carolina Herald and Newsletter Pinckneyville Community of Camden District.

Cheecy, R.B., *The Legend of Betsy Dowdy, North Carolina Booklet, Vol 1, September 1, 1901, No. 5*. Raleigh, North Carolina: Capital Printing Company, 1901.

Caruthers, Rev. E.W. *A Sketch of the Life and Character of the Rev. David Caldwell, D.D.* Greensborough, North Carolina: Swaim and Sherwood, 1842.

Casey, Susan, *Women Heroes of the American Revolution: 20 Stories of Espionage, Sabotage, Defiance, and Rescue.* Chicago, Illinois: Chicago Review Press, 2015.

Claghorn, Charles E., *Women Patriots of the American Revolution: A Biographical Dictionary.* Metuchen, New Jersey: The Scarecrow Press, 1991.

Cook, Bernard, editor, *Women and War: A Historical Encyclopedia from Antiquity to the Present Vol. 2.* Santa Barbara, California: ABC-Clio, 2006.

Coulter, E. Merton, *Nancy Hart, Georgia Heroine of the Revolution: The Story of the Growth of a Tradition,* Georgia Historical Quarterly 39, June 1955.

Custis, George Washington Parke, *Recollections and Private Memories of Washington.* New York, New York:

Derby & Jackson, 1860.

Dacquino, V.T., *Sybil Ludington The Call to Arms.* Fleischmanns, New York: Purple Mountain Press, 2000.

Daigler, Kenneth, A., *Spies, Patriots, and Traitors: American Intelligence in the Revolutionary War.* Washington D.C.: Georgetown Press, 2014.

D.A.R. American Revolution Magazine, Vol 5 July to December, 1895.

D.A.R. American Revolution Magazine, Vol. 17, July-December, 1900.

D.A.R. Magazine Vol. LII, No. 1, January 1918.

D.A.R. American Spirit, Vols. 136-137.

D.A.R. Lineage Book.

D.A.R. North Carolina Society, *The North Carolina Booklet.* Vol. VIII, July, 1908, No. 1.

Deborah Champion, Letter to Patience, October 2, 1775. In the Miscellaneous Manuscripts Collection, Archival Manuscript Material, Library of Congress Manuscript Division, Washington D. C. Reprinted in Lisa Grunwald and Stephen J. Adler, eds. *Women's Letters: America from the Revolutionary War to the Present.*

DePauw, Linda Grant, *Battle Cries and Lullabies.* Norman, Oklahoma: University of Oklahoma Press, 1998.

Diamant, Lincoln, editor, *Revolutionary Women: In the War for American Independence.* Westport, Connecticut: Praeger, 1998.

Dix, Warren R., editor, *Historic Elizabeth 1664-1932.* Elizabeth, New Jersey: Elizabeth Dailey Journal, 1914.

Drisco, George W., *Narrative of the Town of Machias.* Machias, Maine: Geo. A. Parlin, 1904.

Drisko, George W., *The Revolution, Life of Hannah Weston.* Machias, Maine: Geo. A. Parlin, 1903.

Dunlap, John, *The Sentiments of an American Woman.* Pennsylvania: John Dunlap, 1780.

Eaton, Harriet Phillips, *Jersey City and Its Historical Sites.* Jersey City, New Jersey: The Woman's Club, 1899.

Edgar, Walter, editor, *The South Carolina Encyclopedia Guide to the American Revolution in South Carolina.* Columbia, South Carolina: University of South Carolina Press, 2006.

Edwards, Clayton, *A Treasury of Heroes and Heroines: A Record of High Endeavor and Strange Adventure.* New York, New York: Frederick A. Stokes Company, 1920.

Egle, William Henry, editor, *Some Pennsylvania Women during the War of the Revolution.* Harrisburg, Pennsylvania: Harrisburg Publish Co., 1898.

Elizabeth Zane Chapter, West Virginia State Society, D.A. R.

Ellet, Elizabeth, *Women of the Revolution Vol. 1*. Bedford, Massachusetts, 1849.

Endicott, Charles M., *Account of Leslie's Retreat at the North Bridge in Salem*. Salem, Massachusetts: William Ives & George W. Pease Printers, 1856.

Felch, William Farrand, George Atwell, H. Phelps Arms, and Francis Treeyan Miller, *The Connecticut Magazine, Vol. 9*. Hartford and New Haven, Connecticut, 1905.

Fendrick, Virginia Shannon, *American Revolutionary Soldiers of Franklin County, Pennsylvania*. Franklin County, Pennsylvania: Historical Works Committee of the Franklin County Chapter, 1944.

Foster, Sophie Lee, *Revolutionary Reader, Reminiscences and Indian Legends*. Atlanta, Georgia: Byrd Printing Company, 1913.

Frank, Lisa Tendrich, *Encyclopedia of American Women at War: From the Home Front to the Battlefields, Vol 1*. Santa Barbara, California: ABC-CLIO, 2013.

Fremont-Barnes, Gregory editor, *Encyclopedia of the Age of Political Revolutions and New Ideologies, 1760-1815*. Westport, Connecticut: Greenwood Press, 2007.

Gates, Henry Louis Jr. and Evelyn Brooks Higginbotham editors, *African American Lives*. New York, New York: Oxford University Press, 2004.

Grant, Anne, *Danbury's Burning: The Story of Sybil Ludington's Ride*. New York, New York: H.Z. Walck, 1976.

Green, Harry Clinton and Mary Wolcott Green, *The Pioneer Mothers of America*. New York, New York: G.P. Putnam & Sons, 1912.

Green, Theda Michael, *The Columbia Guide to American Indians of the Southeast*. New York, New York: Columbia University Press, 2001.

Hakim, Joy. *From Colonies to Country, 1735-1791*. New York, New York: Oxford University Press, 1993.

Halsey, R.T.H., *The Boston Port Bill as Pictured by a Contemporary London Cartoonist*. New York, New York: The Grolier Club, 1904.

Hannaford, Phebe A. *Daughters of America on Women of the Century*. Boston, Massachusetts: B.B. Russell, 1883.

Harman, John Newton, Jr., *Annals of Tazewell County, Virginia from 1800 to 1922 in Two Volumes*. Richmond, Virginia: W.C. Hill Printing Co., 1922.

Harrell-Sesniak, Mary, *Five Hundred Plus Revolutionary War Obituaries and Death Notices*. Houston, Texas: Lulu, 2010.

_____, *History in the Making*, California State University, San Bernardino Journal of History, Vol. 9.

Hunter, Ryan Ann, *In Disguise! Undercover with Real Women Spies*. New York, New York: Simon & Schuster, 2015.

James, Edward T., *Notable American Women, 1607-1950: A Biographical Dictionary Vol. II*. Cambridge, Massachusetts: Harvard University Press. 1971.

Jarrett, Diane Silcox, *Heroines of the American Revolution: America's Founding Mothers*. Chapel Hill, North Carolina: Green Angel Press, 1998.

Johansen, Bruce Elliot and Barbara Alice Mann, editors, *Encyclopedia of the Haudenosaunee (Iroquois Confederacy)*. Westport, Connecticut: Greenwood Press, 2000.

Johnston, David E., *A History of Middle New River Settlements and Contiguous Territory*. Huntington, West Virginia: Standard Printing and Publishing Co., 1906.

Kate Book. Com, a Website for Kates, by Kates, and About Kates.

Kelly, C. Brian, *Best Little Stories from the American Revolution: More than 100 True Stories*. Naperville, Illinois: Cumberland House: 1999.

Kilmeade, Brian and Don Yaeger, *George Washington's Secret Six: The Spy Ring That Saved the American Revolution*. New York, New York: Penguin Group, 2013.

Kneib, Martha, *Women Soldiers, Spies, and Patriots of the American Revolution*. New York, New York: Rosen Publishing Group, 2004.

Kugel, Rebecca and Lucy Eldersveld Murphy, editors, *Native Women's History in Eastern North America Before 1900*. Lincoln, Nebraska: University of Nebraska Press, 2007.

Landis, John B., *A Short History of Molly Pitcher, the Heroine of the Battle of Monmouth*. Carlisle, Pennsylvania: Cornman Printing, 1903.

Landrum, Dr. John B.O., History of Spartanburg County, South Carolina. Atlanta, Georgia: Franklin Printing & Publishing Co., 1900.

Lee, Richard G., *The American Patriot's Bible*. Nashville, Tennessee: Thomas Nelson Incorporated, 2012.

Leonard, Elizabeth, *All the Daring of the Soldier*. New York, New York: Penguin Books, 2001.

Lewis, Virgil A., *United States Magazine, Vol. III, No. 3, September 1856*.

Lifaro, Michael, *Daniel Boone: An American*. Lexington, Kentucky: University *of Kentucky Press, 2003*.

Lockwood, Estelle D., *The Lady Known as "355"*. West Sayville, New York: Long Island Forum, Winter 1993.

Logan, Mrs. John A., *The Part Taken by Women in America History*. Wilmington, Delaware: The Perry-Nalle Publishing Company, 1912.

Lossing, Benson J. editor, *The Diary of George Washington from 1789 to 1791*. New York, New York: Charles B. Richardson & Co., 1860.

Lossing, Benson J., *A History of the United States from the Discovery of the American Continent to the Present Time*. New York, New York: James Sheehy, 1881.

Lovett, Howard Meriwether, *Grandmother Stories from the Land of Used-to-Be*. Atlanta, Georgia: A.B. Caldwell, 1913.

Mahoney, Harry and Marjorie Locke Mahoney, *Gallantry in Action: A Biographic Dictionary of Espionage in the American Revolutionary War*. Lanham, Maryland: University Press of America, 1999.

Mails Thomas E., The Cherokee People: *The Story of the Cherokees from Earliest Origins to Contemporary Times*. Tulsa, Oklahoma: Council Oak Books, 1992.

Mann, H., *The Female Review: Or, Memoirs of an American Young Lady* by H. Mann, Nathaniel and Benjamin Heaton Printers, 1797.

Mays, Dorothy, *Women in Early America: Struggle, Survival, and Freedom in a New World*. Santa Barbara, California: ABC-CLIO, 2004.

McCullough, David, *Seventeen Seventy-Six*. New York, New York: Simon and Schuster, 2005.

MacDonald, Anne, *No Idle Hands: The Social History of American Knitting*. New York, New York: Ballantine Books, 1988.

McIntosh, John H., *History of Elbert County, Georgia 1790-1935*. Stephen Heard Chapter, Daughters of the American Revolution, 1940.

Meriwether, Colyer, *Publications of the Southern History Association Vol. 1.* Washington D.C.: The Association, 1901.

Misencik, Paul, R., *Sally Townsend, George Washington's Teenage Spy.* Jefferson, North Carolina: McFarland, *2016.*

Morris, George Pope, *The Deserted Bride: and Other Poems.* New York, New York: D. Appleton and Co., 1843.

Mussey, Ellen Spencer, editor, *The American Monthly Magazine D.A.R., Vol. XII, January-June 1898.*

Neimeyer, Charles Patrick, *The Revolutionary War.* Santa Barbara, California: Greenwood Publishing Group, 2007.

New York Times Article 7 December, 1879.

The New York Times, 6 October, 1998.

Obituary, 26 July, 1814 Portsmouth Gazette.

Obituary in Pennsylvania Independent Gazetteer, 2 January, 1790.

Parry, Edward Owen, *Mary Frazer: Heroine of the American Revolution.* D.A.R. Magazine 1984.

Pendleton, William C., *History of Tazewell County and Southwest Virginia 1748-1920.* Richmond, Virginia: W.C. Hill Printing Co., 1920.

Powell, William S., editor, *Dictionary of North Carolina Biography: Vol. 5, P-S,* Chapel Hill, North Carolina: North Carolina Press, 1994.

Raphael, Ray, *A People's History of the American Revolution.* New York, New York: New Press, 2001.

Ricord, R.W., *History of Union County, New Jersey, Vol. 1-2.* Newark, New Jersey: East Jersey History Company. 1897.

Roberts, Cokie, *Founding Mothers The Women Who Raised a Nation.* New York, New York: William Marrow, 2004.

Rockwell, Anne, *They Called Her Molly Pitcher.* Topeka, Kansas: Tandem Library, 2006.

Rosanna Farrow – A Spartanburg County Revolutionary Heroine, an essay by Miss Ruth Petty, Converse College, Class of 1897.

Rose, Alexander, *Washington's Spies: The Story of America's First Spy Ring.* New York, New York: Bantam Dell, 2007.

Rummel, Jack, *African-American Social Leaders and Activists.* New York, New York: Facts on File, Inc., 2003.

Sarnecky, Mary T., *A History of the U.S. Army Nurse Corps.* Philadelphia, Pennsylvania: University of Pennsylvania Press, 1999.

Sawyer, Susan, *More than Petticoats: Remarkable Tennessee Women.* Guilford, Connecticut: Globe Pequot, 2014.

Saye, James Hodge, *Memoirs of Maj. Joseph McLunkin.* Unknown Publisher, South Carolina, 1925.

Scott, John Thomas, *Nancy Hart: Too Good Not to Tell Again in Georgia Women: Their Lives and Times Vol. 1.* Athens, Georgia: University of Georgia Press, 2009.

Sedgwick, Catharine Maria, Slavery in New England Bentley's Miscellany. London: Richard Bentley, 1853.

Seward, Samuel Lee, *The Seward's of Guilford, Connecticut and the Experiences of One of Them from 1848 to 1944.*

Shattuck, Lemuel, *Memorials of the Descendants of William Shattuck.* Boston, Massachusetts: Dutton and Wentworth, 1855.

Shipp, J.E.D., *Giant Days or the Life and Times of William H. Crawford.* Americus, Georgia: Southern Printers, 1908.

Solano, Connie, *Courageous Women: Thirty-Two Short Stories.* Tucson, Arizona: Wheatmark, 2011.

Sons of the American Revolution Magazine, Winter 2014.

Treadway, Sandra, *Anna Maria Lane: An Uncommon Soldier of the American Revolution*. Virginia Cavalcade 37, No. 3, 1988.

Wallis, Thomas L., *Carolina Herald, March 1990.*

Wheeler, John H., *Historical Sketches of North Carolina from 1584 to 1851*. Philadelphia, Pennsylvania: Lippincott, Grambo, & Company, 1851.

Wildwood, Warren, *Thrilling Adventures among the Early Settlers*. Philadelphia, Pennsylvania: J. Edwin Potter, 1866.

Williams, Charles Fish, *Genealogical Notes of the Williams and Gallup Families*. Hartford, Connecticut: Press of the Case, Lockwood, and Brainard Company, 1897.

Wonderley, *Anthony Wayne and Hope Emily Allen, Oneida Iroquois Folklore, Myth, and History: New York Oral Narrative from the Notes of H.E. Allen and Others*. Syracuse, New York: Syracuse University Press, 2004.

Young and Brave: Girls Changing History. Website.

Government Records

Sons of the American Revolution Applications. Ancestry.com database.

American Revolution and War of 1812, Vol. 1. Ancestry.com database.

Boston Marriages from 1752 to 1761. Ancestry.com database.

Census records. Ancestry.com database.

Connecticut Town Birth Records. Ancestry.com database.

Connecticut Town Marriage Records pre-1870. Ancestry.com database.

Index of Obituaries, Massachusetts 1740-1800. Ancestry.com database.

Massachusetts, Wills & Probate Records 1635-1999, Vol. 74-75. Ancestry.com database.

New Hampshire, Death & Burial Records 1654-1949. Ancestry.com database.

New Jersey Marriage Records. Ancestry.com database.

North America, Family Histories, 1500-2000. Ancestry.com database.

Papers of the Continental Congress, National Archives, Washington, D.C.

Pennsylvania in the Revolutionary War 1775-1783. Ancestry.com database.

Pension List of 1792-1795. Ancestry.com database.

Sons of the American Revolution Applications. Ancestry.com database.

U.S. Pension Records. Ancestry.com database.

Vital Records of Haverhill, Massachusetts before 1749. Ancestry.com database.

Index

CPSIA information can be obtained
at www.ICGtesting.com
Printed in the USA
LVHW061136110323
741306LV00010B/118